Name _____

Color Words

Write the color of the fruit or vegetable to complete the puzzle.

Across

3. a carrot

5. a blueberry

6. a strawberry

Down

1. a plum

2. a lemon

4. a lime

D1067241

How Many Toys?

Count. Write the number word for each clue.

Across

2. (three dolls)

3. (four cars)

4. (eight blocks)

6. (seven trucks)

7. (eight figures)

Down

1. (one jump rope)

2. (two balls)

3. (five tops)

5. (ten airplanes)

6. (seven bears)

Word Box

one
two
three
four
five
six
seven
eight
nine
ten

FS-32085 Crossword Puzzles

Counting Clothes

Count. Write the number word for each clue.

Across

2. 👕👕👕👕👕👕👕👕👕👕👕👕👕👕

4. 🩳🩳🩳🩳🩳🩳🩳🩳🩳🩳🩳🩳

Down

1. 🧢🧢🧢🧢🧢🧢🧢🧢🧢🧢🧢🧢

2. 👔👔👔👔👔👔👔👔👔👔👔👔👔👔

3. 👖👖👖👖👖👖👖👖👖👖

Word Box
eleven
twelve
thirteen
fourteen
fifteen

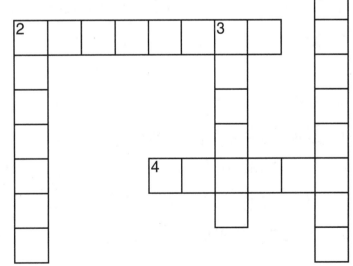

FS-32085 Crossword Puzzles

Name _____

Measurement

Read each sentence and use the words in the Work Box to complete the puzzle.

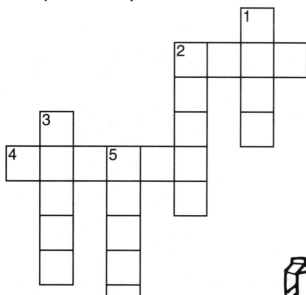

Word Box

gallon	pound
liter	yards
inch	pint

Across

2. Jose ate a _____ of chocolate ice cream.

4. Mom bought a _____ of milk.

Down

1. The inchworm is one _____ long.

2. The cake recipe required a _____ of butter.

3. The length of a football field is 100 _____ .

5. Alfred bought a two _____ bottle of soda.

At the Pet Shop

Read the clues and use the words in the Word Box to complete the puzzle.

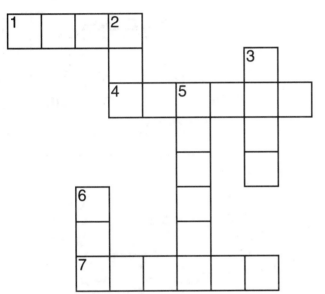

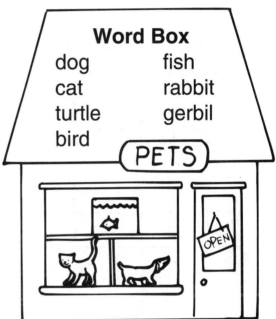

Word Box

dog   fish
cat   rabbit
turtle   gerbil
bird

PETS

OPEN

Across

1. I have feathers.
   I can fly and sing.

4. I am small and furry with a long skinny tail.
   I like running around on a wheel.

7. I have a hard shell.
   I walk very slowly.

Down

2. I have fur.
   I can bark and do tricks.

3. I am very quiet.
   I swim around in a bowl.

5. I have long floppy ears and a fluffy round tail.
   I like eating carrots.

6. I am fluffy and furry.
   When you pet me I purr.

Baby Animals

Find the baby animal for each adult animal to complete the puzzle.

Word Box

chick	fawn
puppy	kitten
foal	tadpole
duckling	calf

Across

3. cow

5. cat

7. dog

8. duck

Down

1. horse

2. hen

4. deer

6. frog

Name _____

Animal Coverings

Find the type of covering for each animal to complete the puzzle.

Word Box

shell	quills
fur	feathers
skin	scales

Across

1. snow hare
3. elephant
5. goldfish

Down

1. swan
2. porcupine
3. turtle

FS-32085 Crossword Puzzles

Dinosaurs

Read the sentences and use the words in the Word Box to complete the puzzle.

Word Box

plates	horns
meat	lizard
tail	

Across

3. The name Brontosaurus means "thunder _____."

4. A Tyrannosaurus was the largest _____-eating dinosaur.

Down

1. A Triceratops had three _____ and a massive shield.

2. A Stegosaurus had huge bony _____ along its back.

5. An Ankylosaurus had a heavy club at the end of its _____.

Name _____

Mammals

Read the clues and use the words in the Word Box to complete the puzzle.

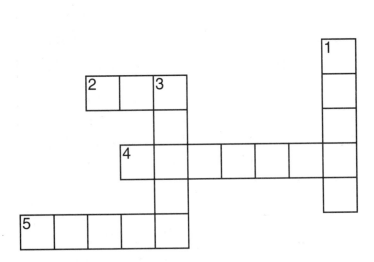

Word Box
raccoon
skunk
mouse
cow
whale

Across

2. I live on a farm and give people milk.

4. I look like I wear a mask.

5. I am very small and have a long skinny tail.

Down

1. I am black with a white stripe going down the middle of my back.

3. I live in the ocean.

 FS-32085 Crossword Puzzles

Name _____

Amphibians and Reptiles

Read the sentences and use the words in the Word Box to complete the puzzle.

Word Box
amphibian
reptile
turtle
crocodile
frog

Across

2. A _____ is a reptile that has a shell and pulls its head, legs, and tail into the shell for protection.

3. An _____ is a cold-blooded animal that has scaleless skin and lives part of its life in water.

5. A _____ is a reptile that has a long snout.

Down

1. A _____ is a cold-blooded animal that has dry, scaly skin.

4. A _____ is an amphibian that has four legs and no tail.

FS-32085 Crossword Puzzles

Name _____

Parts of a Plant

Read the clues and use the words in the Word Box to complete the puzzle.

Word Bank
leaves
stem
roots
fruit
seeds
flower

Across

3. They make food for the plant.

4. New plants grow from these.

5. This covers and protects the seeds.

Down

1. These take in water and minerals from the soil.

2. This is the part where the seeds are formed.

4. It carries the water and minerals to the leaves.

FS-32085 Crossword Puzzles

Name _____

Plants We Eat

Read the sentences and use the words in the Word Box to complete the puzzle.

Word Box
carrot
rhubarb
lettuce
corn
peach

Across

2. When we eat a _____, we are eating the fruit of a plant.

4. When we eat _____, we are eating the leaves of a plant.

5. When we eat _____, we are eating the seeds of a plant.

Down

1. When we eat a _____, we are eating the root of a plant.

3. When we eat _____, we are eating the stem of a plant.

FS-32085 Crossword Puzzles

Living Things

Read the clues and use the words in the tree to complete the puzzle.

girl
flower
tree
eagle
fish
elephant

Across

2. I can fly.

3. I am a plant.
   I have petals and smell pretty.

4. I have a trunk, leaves, and branches.

Down

1. I am a person.

2. I am a large gray animal with a long trunk and big, floppy ears.

3. I live in the water and can swim.

FS-32085 Crossword Puzzles

Nonliving Things

Read the sentences and use the words in the Word Box to complete the puzzle.

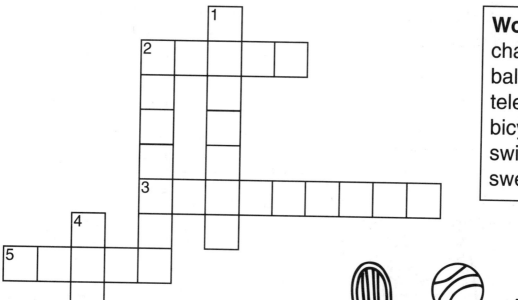

Word Box
chair
ball
telephone
bicycle
swing
sweater

Across

2. A _____ is something you play on.

3. A _____ is something you call people on to talk to them.

5. A _____ is something that has four legs and you sit on it.

Down

1. A _____ is something you ride on that has two wheels.

2. A _____ is something you wear to keep you warm.

4. A _____ is something you can throw and catch.

Name _____

Fishes

Read the sentences and use the words in the Word Box to complete the puzzle.

Word Box

colors   ocean
lakes   fins
mouths   gills

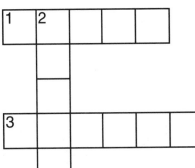

Across

1. Saltwater fish live in the _____.

3. Fish open and close their _____ as they swim to get air from the water.

4. The water comes out of their _____.

6. Fish have tails and _____.

Down

2. Fish are many different sizes, shapes, and _____.

5. Freshwater fish live in ponds, rivers, or _____.

    FS-32085 Crossword Puzzles

Name _____

Forest Life

Read the sentences and use the words in the Word Box to complete the puzzle.

Word Box

sunlight	forest
insects	trees
squirrels	deer

Across

3. _____ climb trees and eat acorns.

5. Many _____ crawl along the forest floor.

6. Many _____ grow in the forest.

Down

1. A little bit of _____ shines through the trees.

2. It is cool and dark in the _____ .

4. A _____ nibbles on the sweet green plants.

Desert Life

Read the sentences and use the words in the Word Box to complete the puzzle.

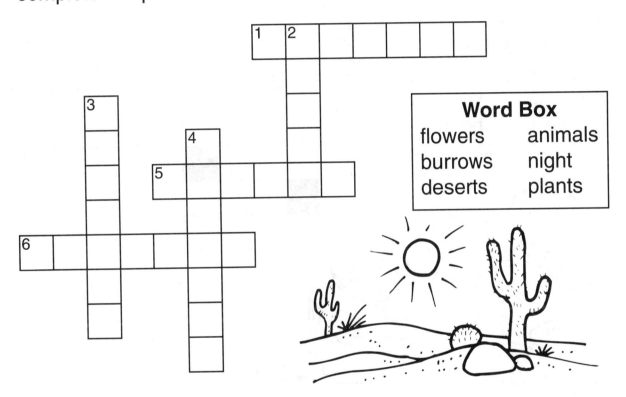

Word Box

flowers	animals
burrows	night
deserts	plants

Across

1. Desert ____ get water from the food they eat.

5. Desert ____ store water in their leaves, roots, or stems.

6. Many small animals stay in ____ underground during the day.

Down

2. At ____ , the desert animals begin to stir.

3. ____ are very hot and get little rainfall.

4. After it rains, colorful ____ bloom across the desert.

FS-32085 Crossword Puzzles

At the Pond

Read the sentences and use the words in the Word Box to complete the puzzle.

Word Box

cattails	fish
lily pad	willow
turtle	pond

Across

4. A bullfrog sits on a _____ and croaks a loud song.

5. A family of ducks waddle into the _____ for a swim.

6. A raccoon tries to catch a _____ as it swims by.

Down

1. A _____ sits on a rock in the morning sun.

2. The weeping _____ gives shade to the animals.

3. Birds fly over the many _____ sticking out of the water.

Name _____

Land and Water

Read the clues and use the words in the Word Box to complete the puzzle.

Word Box
mountain
valley
plain
ocean
lake
river

Across

2. This is a body of fresh water surrounded by land.

4. This is a very high hill.

6. This is low land between mountains or hills.

Down

1. This is a very flat stretch of land.

3. This is a flowing stream of water.

5. This is a large body of salt water.

FS-32085 Crossword Puzzles

Magnets

Read the sentences and use the words in the Word Box to complete the puzzle.

Word Box
bar
paper clip
poles
eraser
horseshoe
ring

Across

2. This is a ____ magnet.

4. A magnet will attract a ____ .

6. A magnet will not attract an ____ .

Down

1. This is a ____ magnet.

3. This is a ____ magnet.

5. The ____ are at the ends of a magnet.

Name _____

Solids, Liquids, Gases

Read the sentences and use the words in the Word Box to complete the puzzle.

Word Box
solid
liquid
gas
water
wagon
air

Across

1. A liquid you can drink is _____.

2. A _____ does not have a shape of its own, and it spreads out to fill the container it is in.

5. A _____ can be poured and takes the shape of the container it is in.

Down

1. A _____ is a solid.

3. A _____ keeps its shape.

4. A gas you breathe is _____ .

FS-32085 Crossword Puzzles

Being a Friend

Read the sentences and use the words in the Word Box to complete the puzzle.

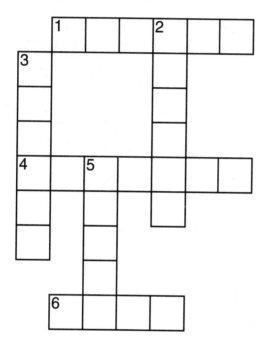

Word Box
respect
fairly
help
share
follow
listen

Across

1. You should ____ the rules.

4. Try to ____ others' feelings.

6. Always ____ others.

Down

2. You should ____ when others are talking.

3. You should treat others ____.

5. Try to ____ with others.

FS-32085 Crossword Puzzles

Feelings

Look at the picture clues and use the words in the Word Box to complete the puzzle.

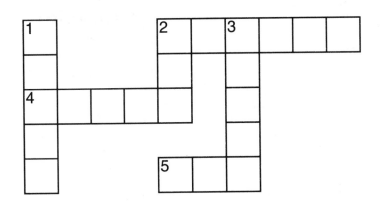

Word Box
happy
sad
shy
scared
proud
angry

Across

2.

4.

5.

Down

1.

2.

3.

FS-32085 Crossword Puzzles

Healthy Foods

Read the sentences and use the words in the Word Box to complete the puzzle.

Word Box
fruit
vegetable
bread
milk
meat

Across

2. A bagel is a food from the _____ and cereal group.

3. A slice of cheese belongs to the _____ group.

4. An orange is a food from the _____ group.

Down

1. Broccoli is a food from the _____ group.

3. Chicken and eggs belong to the _____ group.

Name _____

A Neighborhood

Read the sentences and use the words in the Word Box to complete the puzzle.

Word Box
house
street
school
store
sidewalk
park

Across

1. The children go to _____ .

4. Latasha and Ryan walked on the _____ .

5. Mom and Dad went to the_____ to buy groceries.

Down

2. Tyana lives in the blue _____ on the corner.

3. The children play in the _____.

4. Cars drive up and down the _____ .

FS-32085 Crossword Puzzles

In a City

Read the clues and use the words in the Word Box to complete the puzzle.

Word Box

subway	taxi
skyscraper	mall
hospital	bus
museum	zoo

Across

2. This is a place with many stores in one building.
3. This is a place where many animals live.
4. This is a very tall building.
6. Many people ride in this on city streets.
7. People whistle, yell, or wave to get a ride in this thing.

Down

1. This is a place where people go when they are very sick.
2. People visit this place to see very old things.
5. This train goes underground and many people ride on it.

Safety

Read the clues and use the words in the Word Box to complete the puzzle

Word Box
seat belt
helmet
life jacket
stop sign
traffic light

Across

4. I tell cars when to stop and go.

5. I help you keep afloat when you are in the water.

Down

1. I am red with white letters. I sit on a post.

2. You wear me on your head when you ride a bike.

3. You wear me when you ride in a car.

FS-32085 Crossword Puzzles

Fire Safety

Read the sentences and use the words in the Word Box to complete the puzzle.

Word Box

breathe	shout
opening	roll
call	calm

Across

2. Feel the door first before _____ it.
3. Stay low, close to the floor, to _____ the cleaner air.
6. You should _____ 9-1-1 immediately.

Down

1. You can _____ loudly to let people know there's a fire.
4. Stop, drop, and _____ if your clothing is on fire.
5. Stay _____.

FS-32085 Crossword Puzzles

Firefighters

Read the sentences and use the words in the Word Box to complete the puzzle.

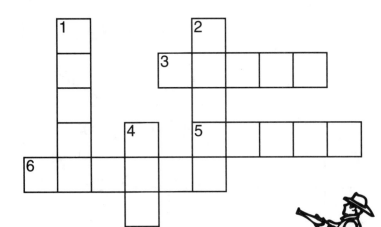

Word Box

engine	slide
house	fight
clean	coats

Across

3. They put on their _____ , boots, and helmets.

5. As the fire alarm goes off, the firefighters _____ down the nearest fire pole.

6. They jump onto the fire _____ .

Down

1. They check, _____ , and put away all of their equipment.

2. After the fire is put out, the firefighters go back to the fire _____ .

4. They turn on their siren and speed away to _____ the fire.

Things That Are Alike

Read the clues and find the other things from the Word Box that go with each group to complete the puzzle.

Word Box

volleyball   spoon

turtle   truck

crayon   turkey

Across

1. pizza   sandwich

3. car   motorcycle

5. basketball   baseball

Down

1. dog   cat

2. knife   fork

4. pencil   marker

FS-32085 Crossword Puzzles

Rhyming Puzzle

Read each clue and find the rhyming word for the word in **dark print** to complete the puzzle.

Word Box

blocks	fair
plane	swing
flower	moon
bee	name

Across

2. It's going to **rain**.
   I'm flying in a _____.

4. You eat with a **spoon**.
   There is a full _____.

5. I climbed a **tree**.
   I was stung by a _____.

6. There's a chance of a rain **shower**. Sue has a red _____.

Down

1. Maria has a **ring**.
   I played on the _____.

3. Did you play a **game**.
   What is your _____?

5. Sue lost her **socks**.
   Mike played with the _____.

6. I'll cut my **hair**.
   Ben saw a pig at the county _____.

FS-32085 Crossword Puzzles

Months of the Year

Read the clues. Use the words in the Word Box to complete the puzzle.

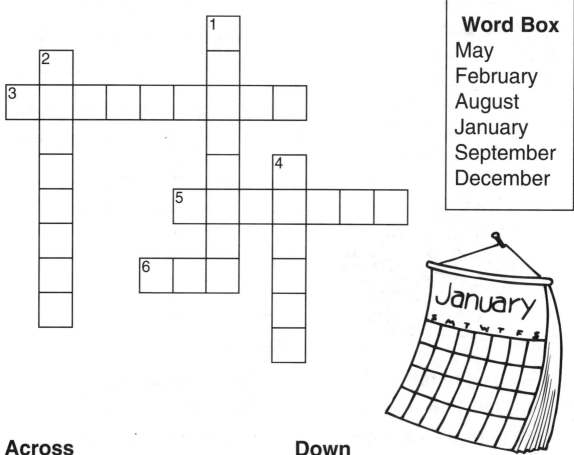

Word Box
May
February
August
January
September
December

Across

3. This is the month before October.

5. This is the first month of the year.

6. This is the month after April.

Down

1. This is the month that has the least number of days.

2. This is the last month of the year.

4. This is the month between July and September.

FS-32085 Crossword Puzzles

Animal Alphabet

Write each group of words in ABC order.
Write the words in the puzzle.

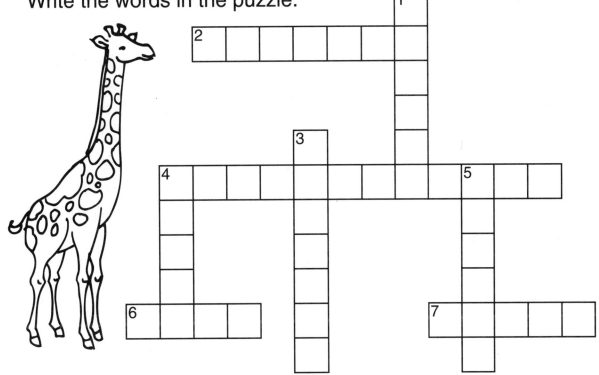

Across

zebra   seal
hippopotamus   giraffe

Down

monkey   gorilla
horse   ferret

2._____   1._____

4._____   3._____

6._____   4._____

7._____   5._____

FS-32085 Crossword Puzzles

Find the Nouns

Nouns are words that name a person, place, or thing.
Read each clue and find the noun to complete the puzzle.

Word Box

artist	umbrella
chef	house
baby	flower
playground	bicycle
beach	pencil

Across

1. You use this when it rains.
4. You ride on this.
7. You write with this.
8. This person draws pictures.
9. This is a place where people live.

Down

2. This is a small child.
3. This is a place where children play.
4. This is a place where people build sandcastles.
5. This person cooks.
6. This plant smells pretty.

Lights, Camera, Action

A **verb** is an action word. It tells what the noun in the sentence does or is doing. Read each sentence and find the verb to complete the puzzle.

Word Box
cheers
caught
laughs
kicked
draws
drank
walked
knocks

Across

2. Kalia _____ the baseball.

3. Sonja _____ the soccer ball into the goal.

7. Gina _____ on the door.

8. Andre _____ at the clown.

Down

1. We _____ along the beach.

4. Joaquin _____ for his favorite football player.

5. Sylvia _____ a glass of water.

6. Paula _____ a picture.

Adjective Puzzle

An **adjective** tells or describes more about the noun. Read each clue and find the adjective that best describes the noun.

Word Box

beautiful	juicy
young	soft
fluffy	salty
funny	thick

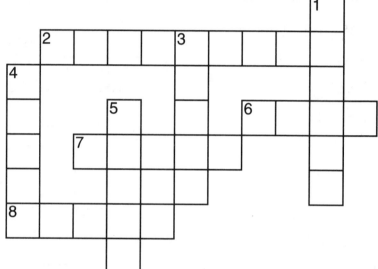

Across

2. _____ flower

6. _____ pillow

7. _____ orange

8. _____ child

Down

1. _____ kitten

3. _____ milk shake

4. _____ pickle

5. _____ clown

FS-32085 Crossword Puzzles

Contraction Puzzle

A **contraction** is two words written as one with an apostrophe taking the place of the missing letters. Read each clue and find the words for the contraction in **dark print**.

Word Box
I am
she will
we have
he is
is not
they would
they are
they have

Across

3. **He's** having a party.
4. **They're** going to the movies.
6. **She'll** fix the car.
7. **We've** been swimming in the lake.

Down

1. **I'm** thirsty.
2. **They'd** like to be in the school play.
4. I think **they've** moved.
5. Bryan **isn't** tired.

FS-32085 Crossword Puzzles

Abbreviations

Read each clue. Find the word in the Word Box for the abbreviation to complete the puzzle.

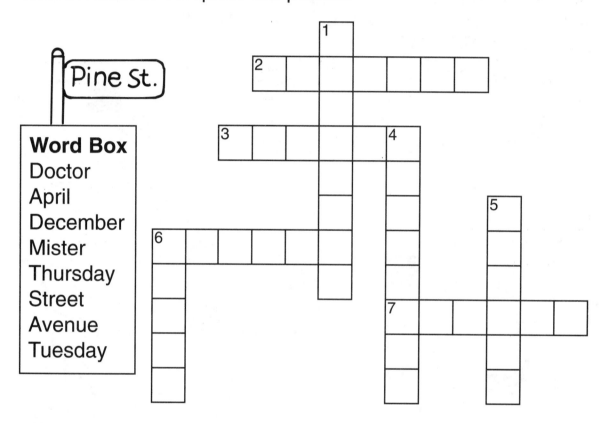

Pine St.

Word Box
Doctor
April
December
Mister
Thursday
Street
Avenue
Tuesday

Across

2. We go to art class on **Tues.**

3. Bill lives on Main **St.**

6. Turn left on Palm **Ave.**

7. **Dr.** Smith is on vacation.

Down

1. It sometimes snows in **Dec.**

4. Kiel has ballet class on **Thurs.**

5. **Mr.** Peters went to the dentist.

6. In **Apr.** the flowers bloom.

FS-32085 Crossword Puzzles

Name _____

On a Farm

Read the sentences and use the words in the Word Box to complete the puzzle.

Word Box
farmer
pigpen
tractor
chicken coop
barn
haystack

Across

3. A pile of hay is called a
   _____.

5. Chickens lay eggs in a
   _____.

6. Cows and horses live in a
   _____.

Down

1. Pigs live in a _____.

2. A person who works on a
   farm is a _____.

4. Something the farmer
   drives is a _____.

FS-32085 Crossword Puzzles

Name _____

Animal Homes

Use the clues to complete the puzzle.

Word Box

spider	prairie dog	woodpecker
beaver	bear	honeybee

Across

4. My home is a burrow.

5. My home is a web.

6. My home is a den.

Down

1. My home is a hive.

2. My home is a lodge.

3. My home is a hole in a tree.

FS-32085 Crossword Puzzles

How Animals Move

Tell how each animal moves to complete the puzzle.

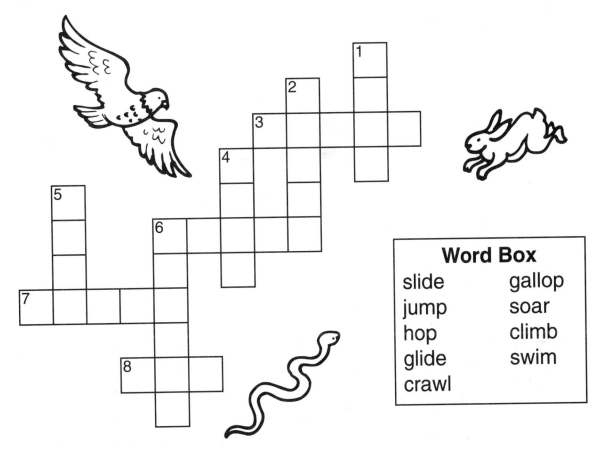

Word Box

slide	gallop
jump	soar
hop	climb
glide	swim
crawl	

Across

3. billy goats
6. pelicans
7. snails
8. rabbits

Down

1. frogs
2. snakes
4. dolphins
5. eagles
6. horses

FS-32085 Crossword Puzzles

Name _____

Animal Groups

Read the clues and use the words in the Word Box to complete the puzzle.

Word Box

fish	bees
pigeons	wolves
elephants	prairie dogs

Across

1. a colony of ____

5. a town of ____

6. a flock of ____

Down

2. a herd of ____

3. a school of ____

4. a pack of ____

FS-32085 Crossword Puzzles

Name _____

Tools and Machines

Read the clues and use the words in the Word Box to complete the puzzle.

Word Box
hammer
lawn mower
washing machine
saw
refrigerator
computer

Across

4. washes clothes

5. helps you learn

6. pounds nails

Down

1. keeps food cold

2. cuts grass

3. cuts wood

FS-32085 Crossword Puzzles

Name _____

At the Beach

Read the sentences and use the words
in the Word Box to complete the puzzle.

Word Box
ocean
seashells
umbrella
sandcastle
shovel
beachball

Across

2. My family sat under the
   beach ____ and ate lunch.
4. At the beach, I built a

   ____ .
6. We saw dolphins
   swimming in the ____ .

Down

1. I took a walk along the
   shore to look for ____ .
3. My brother and I tossed
   the ____ .
5. I used my pail and ____ to
   build a sandcastle.

Keeping Healthy

Read the sentences and use the words in the Word Box to complete the puzzle.

Word Box

exercise   eat
sleep   brush
safety rules   bath
comb

Across

2. Take a _____.

3. You should _____ your muscles.

6. Remember to _____ your teeth.

7. Always _____ healthy foods.

Down

1. Follow the _____ _____.

4. Brush or _____ your hair.

5. Get plenty of _____.

FS-32085 Crossword Puzzles

Community Helpers

Read the clues and use the words in the Word Box to complete the puzzle.

Word Box

firefighter   teacher
police officer doctor
mail carrier   dentist

Across

2. I deliver packages to homes almost every day.

5. You come to me for help when you are lost.

6. I help you learn.

Down

1. I drive a long, red truck with ladders and hoses.

3. You visit me when your tooth hurts.

4. Sometimes you visit me when you are sick.

FS-32085 Crossword Puzzles

People Who Work At Night

Read the sentences and use the words in the Word Box to complete the puzzle.

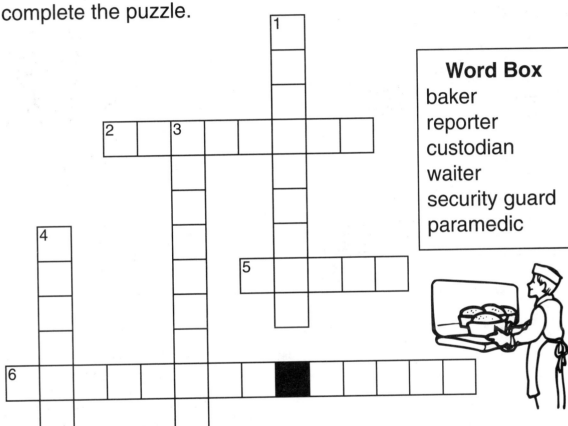

Word Box
baker
reporter
custodian
waiter
security guard
paramedic

Across

2. A _____ writes news stories for newspapers.

5. A _____ makes fresh bread and rolls.

6. A _____ protects buildings.

Down

1. A _____ cleans offices and schools.

3. A _____ drives an ambulance and helps people when they are sick.

4. A _____ serves people food in a restaurant.

FS-32085 Crossword Puzzles

Addition Fun

Add. Write the number word for each answer in the puzzle.

Word Box

one	two
three	four
five	six
seven	eight
nine	ten

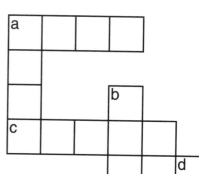

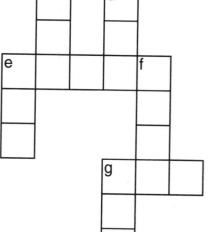

Across

a. 2
 +2

c. 5
 +3

e. 3
 +4

g. 6
 +4

Down

a. 3
 +2

b. 2
 +1

d. 0
 +1

e. 4
 +2

f. 7
 +2

g. 1
 +1

FS-32085 Crossword Puzzles

Subtraction Fun

Subtract. Write the number word for each answer in the puzzle.

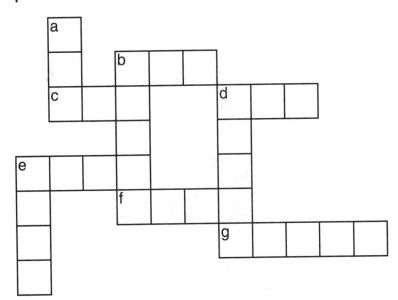

Word Box

one	two
three	four
five	six
seven	eight
nine	ten

Across

b. 9
  − 3

c. 5
  − 4

d. 10
  − 0

e. 7
  − 2

f. 15
  − 6

g. 17
  − 9

Down

a. 6
  − 4

b. 14
  − 7

d. 8
  − 5

e. 12
  − 8

FS-32085 Crossword Puzzles

Addition Puzzle

Solve each addition problem. Write the answers in the puzzle.

863	794
496	439
571	746
266	756
823	968

Across

b. 350
+221

d. 423
+323

f. 324
+115

i. 135
+131

j. 522
+341

Down

a. 522
+234

c. 652
+142

e. 375
+121

g. 644
+324

h. 202
+621

FS-32085 Crossword Puzzles

Subtraction Puzzle

Solve each addition problem. Write the answers in the puzzle.

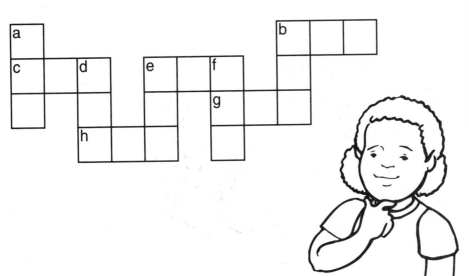

423	641
654	254
362	356
312	434
123	571

Across

b. 978	c. 795	e. 765	g. 895	h. 786
−324	−672	−342	−324	−532

Down

a. 526	b. 875	d. 884	e. 879	f. 799
−214	−234	−522	−445	−443

FS-32085 Crossword Puzzles

Fun With Tens

Read each number and find the number word to complete the puzzle.

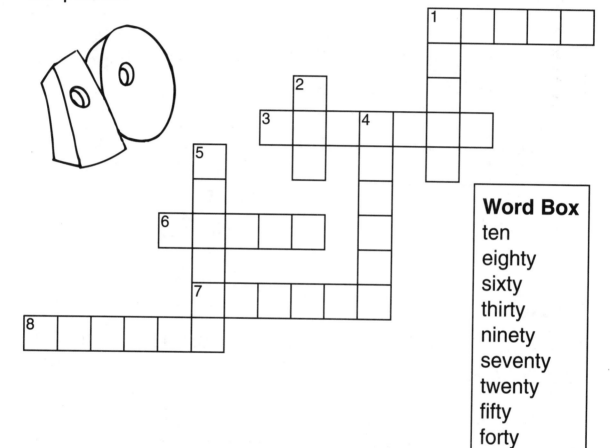

Word Box
ten
eighty
sixty
thirty
ninety
seventy
twenty
fifty
forty

Across

1. 50
3. 70
6. 60
7. 20
8. 90

Down

1. 40
2. 10
4. 80
5. 30

52

At the Zoo

Read the clues. Write the names of the zoo animals in the crossword puzzle.

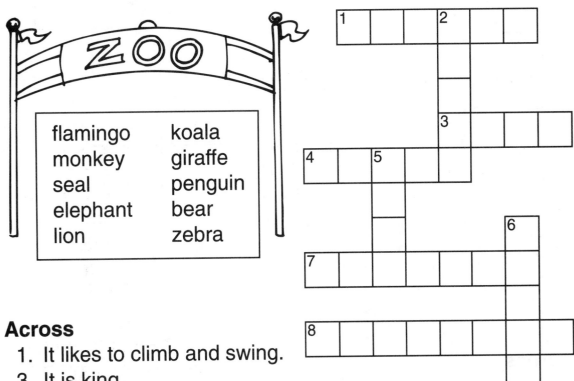

flamingo   koala
monkey   giraffe
seal   penguin
elephant   bear
lion   zebra

Across
1. It likes to climb and swing.
3. It is king.
4. It has black and white stripes.
7. It has a very long neck.
8. It has pink feathers.
10. It has a long, long nose.

Down
2. It eats tasty leaves.
5. It has a big fur coat.
6. It lives where it is icy cold.
9. It loves to play and swim in the water.

FS-32085 Crossword Puzzles

On the Farm

Read the clues. Write the names of the farm animals in the crossword puzzle.

pig
goose
sheep
chicken
horse
rooster
duck
cow
mule

Across

2. It is a good swimmer.
4. It can take you for a ride.
8. It goes "cock-a-doodle-doo."
9. This animal likes the mud.

Down

1. This animal is half donkey and half horse.
3. It lays eggs for the farmer's breakfast.
5. This animal's coat gives us wool.
6. A bird with a long neck and white feathers.
7. She gives milk.

FS-32085 Crossword Puzzles

Bugs, Bugs, Bugs

Read the clues. Write the names of the bugs.

wasp
fly
ant
ladybug
cricket
bee
butterfly
caterpillar

Across

1. This is an insect that makes honey.
4. This bug may change into a butterfly.
5. This bug flies around garbage.
6. She wears a red coat with black spots.

Down

1. This bug has beautifully-colored wings.
2. You might hear this bug chirp at night.
3. This stinging insect makes a paper nest.
7. This worker might like your picnic lunch.

Weather Watch

Read the clues. Write the weather words in the puzzle.

rain
thunder
tornado
wind
sunshine
cloud
storm
lightning
hurricane
fog

Across

1. This is a strong wind with rain or snow.
5. It is a very strong storm with high winds.
7. You might see a puffy white one in the sky.
8. A loud noise after a flash of lightning.
10. When there are no clouds, you will see this.

Down

2. This is drops of water falling from the clouds.
3. It is a twisting whirlwind.
4. This is a flash of electricity in the sky.
6. This is a mist close to the ground.
9. It is moving air.

My Body

Read the clues. Write the parts of the body in the puzzle.

lungs
heart
brain
muscles
stomach
bones
skin
blood
vein

Across

2. These help you breathe.
6. This is where food is digested.
8. It helps you learn and think.

Down

1. These help you move your body.
3. This covers the outside of the body.
4. These make up your skeleton.
5. It is a tube that carries blood to the heart.
7. This pumps blood through your body.
8. This is red liquid in the body.

FS-32085 Crossword Puzzles

The Ocean

Read the clues. Write the ocean words in the puzzle.

whale   dolphin   diver   lobster

shark   jellyfish   oyster   octopus

Across

3. This animal breathes air and looks like a small whale.
5. This animal lives in a shell.
6. This is a dangerous fish that eats other fish.
7. This ocean animal has eight arms.

Down

1. This mammal looks like a huge fish.
2. It looks like jelly and can sometimes sting.
3. This is a person who dives into the ocean.
4. It has big claws on its front legs.

     FS-32085 Crossword Puzzles

Five Senses

Read the clues. Write the words in the crossword puzzle.

see
eyes
hear
ears
taste
mouth
touch
hands
smell
nose

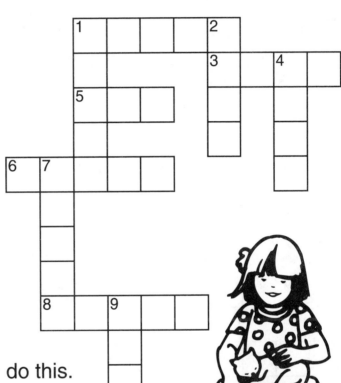

Across

1. Your hands help you do this.
3. You look at a pretty butterfly with these.
5. Your eyes help you do this.
6. You use your nose to do this.
8. You use these to touch a soft kitten.

Down

1. Your mouth helps you do this.
2. Your ears help you do this.
4. You listen to music with these.
7. You taste your favorite fruit with this.
8. You use this to smell a flower.

FS-32085 Crossword Puzzles

In Space

Read the clues. Write the space words in the puzzle.

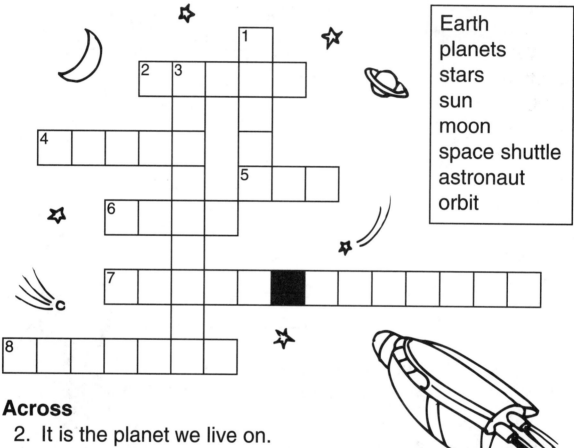

Earth
planets
stars
sun
moon
space shuttle
astronaut
orbit

Across

2. It is the planet we live on.
4. It is the path Earth takes around the sun.
5. This warms Earth and gives it light.
6. It goes around Earth and we see it at night.
7. Astronauts ride this into space.
8. Nine of these go around the sun.

Down

1. There are many of these in the night sky.
3. Someone who travels in space.

FS-32085 Crossword Puzzles

Compound Word Fun

Read the clues. Write the compound words in the puzzle.

seashore
rainbow
footprints
sailboat
watermelon
sunburn
sandcastle

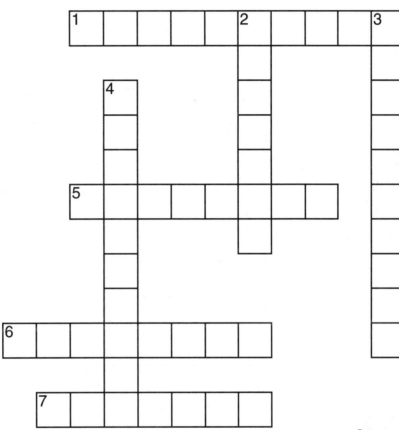

Across
1. Your feet make these in the sand.
5. You can swim here.
6. The wind helps this boat move.
7. You don't want to get this at the beach.

Down
2. Look for this in the sky after it rains.
3. You can build one of these in the sand.
4. This tastes good on a hot day.

FS-32085 Crossword Puzzles

Words With *ch, sh, th,* and *wh*

Read the clues. Write the words in the puzzle.

chick
shower
think
whale
cherry
shade
thirteen
white

Across
1. Clouds can be this color.
3. This hatches from an egg.
4. You do this with your brain.
5. It is a spray of water.
6. It is a very big sea mammal.
7. It is a red fruit.

Down
2. The number after twelve.
5. You may find this under a tree.

"S" Blends

Read the clues. Write the words with "s" blends in the puzzle.

score
swim
skate
snake
slide
stars
spoon
smile

Across

1. You glide down this on a playground.
2. Use this to eat your soup.
4. It is a boot with wheels.
6. This is fun to do in a pool.

Down

1. It is a long, thin animal without legs.
2. Keep track of points in a game.
3. These shine in the sky at night.
5. What you do when you are happy.

Homophones Sound Alike

Read the clues. Write the homophones in the puzzle.

ate	eight
two	too
dear	deer
tail	tale
sale	sail

Across

2. A boat can have this.
3. This animal lives in the forest.
5. What you did at lunchtime.
7. This number is one less than three.
8. A squirrel has a long, furry one.

Down

1. This is what you say at the beginning of a letter.
2. A store can have a sign that says this.
4. This is one more than seven.
6. It is a word that means *also*.
7. This is a story.

FS-32085 Crossword Puzzles

Opposites

Read the clues. Write the opposites in the crossword puzzle.

| clean |
| wet |
| empty |
| over |
| inside |
| under |
| outside |
| full |
| dry |
| dirty |

Across
2. It is the opposite of *under.*
4. It is the opposite of *empty.*
6. It is the opposite of *clean.*
7. It is the opposite of *outside.*
8. It is the opposite of *full.*

Down
1. It is the opposite of *dry.*
2. It is the opposite of *inside.*
3. It is the opposite of *dirty.*
5. It is the opposite of *over.*
6. It is the opposite of *wet.*

FS-32085 Crossword Puzzles

Long Vowels

Read the clues. Write the long vowel words in the puzzle.

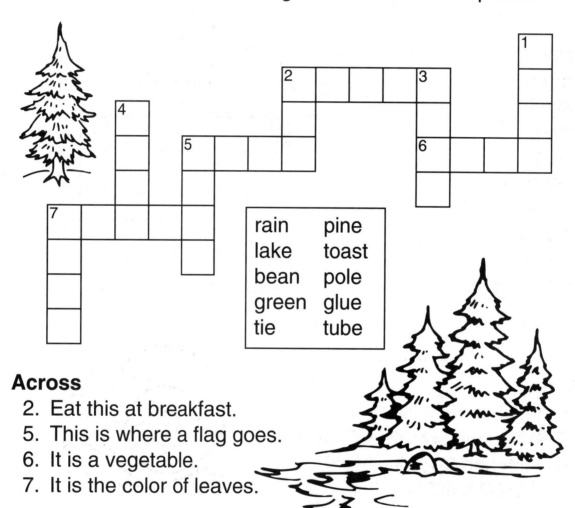

rain	pine
lake	toast
bean	pole
green	glue
tie	tube

Across
  2. Eat this at breakfast.
  5. This is where a flag goes.
  6. It is a vegetable.
  7. It is the color of leaves.

Down
  1. It is water dropping from clouds.
  2. This is what you do to shoelaces.
  3. This is what toothpaste comes in.
  4. It is fun to swim here.
  5. It is a green tree.
  7. This will make things stick.

FS-32085 Crossword Puzzles

Short Vowels

Read the clues. Write the short vowel words in the puzzle.

ranch
grass
shell
desk
clock
pond
thick
picnic
puzzle
drum

Across
2. A lawn has this.
3. Eat lunch outside on a blanket.
5. Fish and frogs live here.
8. A snail has one.
9. You can do your schoolwork here.

Down
1. This is a big farm where cattle are raised.
3. It has lots of pieces to put together.
4. This tells time.
6. This keeps the beat in music.
7. It is the opposite of *thin*.

FS-32085 Crossword Puzzles

Name _____

Parts of a Book

Read the clues. Write the parts of a book in the puzzle.

title	pages
author	words
illustrator	pictures
publisher	cover
date	jacket

Across

5. This is a person who draws the pictures.
7. This is the name of the book.
9. The pieces of paper in a book.
10. The writing in a book.

Down

1. The year the book was made.
2. The drawings or photos in a book.
3. The company that made the book.
4. The outside front and back of the book.
6. The person who wrote the book.
8. A paper cover on the outside of a book.

FS-32085 Crossword Puzzles

Name _____

Frog and Toad Together

Have you read the book *Frog and Toad Together* by Arnold Lobel? Read the clues. Write the words from the story in the crossword puzzle.

list
wind
garden
seeds
cookies
birds
brave
dream
wonderful

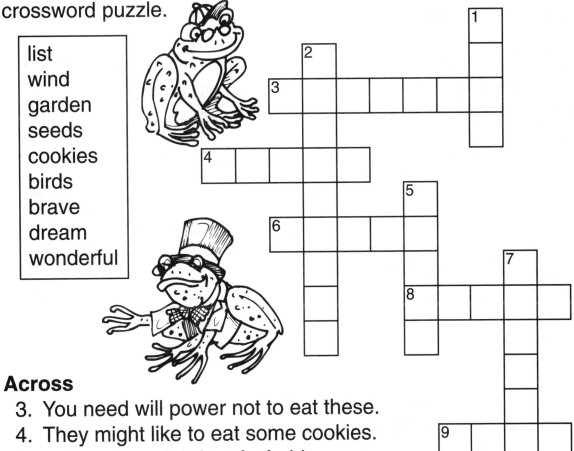

Across
3. You need will power not to eat these.
4. They might like to eat some cookies.
6. This is the opposite of *afraid.*
8. This is what Toad did when he was sleeping.
9. This can blow away your list of things to do.

Down
1. This is something you write.
2. What you might call the greatest toad in all the world.
5. These take some time to grow into flowers.
7. This is where you plant seeds.

FS-32085 Crossword Puzzles

The Gingerbread Man

Do you know the story of The Gingerbread Man? Read the clues. Write the words from the story in the puzzle.

old
fox
oven
woman
kitchen
door
fast
farmers

Across
1. He ate the gingerbread man.
4. It is the opposite of young.
6. This is where the woman baked the gingerbread man.
7. The oven is in this room.

Down
1. They ran after the gingerbread man.
2. She baked the gingerbread man.
3. This is how the gingerbread man ran.
5. The boy opened this.

Name _____

Blueberries for Sal

Have you read the book *Blueberries for Sal* by Robert McCloskey? Read the clues. Write the words from the story in the crossword puzzle.

blueberries
mother
picking
tired
hustle
noise
bear
behind

Across
2. Someone who has a child.
5. You can pick these and put them in a pail.
7. How you might feel after picking berries.

Down
1. It is a sound berries make in a pail.
3. It is a word that means *to go quickly.*
4. Gathering berries.
5. This is an animal that likes to eat berries.
6. It is the opposite of *in front.*

FS-32085 Crossword Puzzles

Name _____

Nursery Rhymes

Read the clues. Write the nursery rhyme words in the puzzle.

clock
lamb
hill
sheep
shoe
fiddle
horn
well
corner

Across

2. Jack and Jill went up the _____.
4. One, two, buckle my _____.
6. Ding, dong, bell, Pussy's in the _____.
8. Little Jack Horner sat in the _____.

Down

1. Hey! diddle, diddle, The cat and the _____.
3. Mary had a little _____.
4. Little Bo-peep has lost her _____.
5. Hickory, dickory, dock, The mouse ran up the _____.
7. Little Boy Blue, Come blow your _____.

FS-32085 Crossword Puzzles

Name _____

Beauty and the Beast

Do you know the story of Beauty and the Beast? Read the clues. Write the words from the story in the puzzle.

rose
father
castle
mirror
library
marry
ring
prince
happy

Across
4. Beauty had one of these that was filled with books.
6. The Beast changed into a handsome one.
8. Beauty missed her home and this person.
9. Father picked one from the Beast's garden.

Down
1. The Beast loved Beauty and asked her to do this.
2. At the end of the story, Beauty feels like this.
3. When you look in this you see yourself.
5. The Beast gave Beauty a magic one to wear on her finger.
7. This is where a prince lives.

     FS-32085 Crossword Puzzles

The Elves and the Shoemaker

Do you know the story of the Elves and the Shoemaker?
Read the clues. Write the words from the story in the puzzle.

shoemaker
wife
midnight
elves
clothes
leather
hammer
work

Across

2. The shoemaker's wife made these for the elves to wear.
4. The elves came at this time of night.
5. The shoemaker cut this to make shoes.
6. This is the opposite of *play*.
7. These are magical little people.

Down

1. This is a tool for making shoes.
3. This is a person who makes shoes.
6. The shoemaker was married to her.

FS-32085 Crossword Puzzles

The Three Bears

Do you know the story of the Three Bears? Read the clues.
Write the words from the story in the puzzle.

little
middle
big
porridge
hot
chair
bed
sleep
woods

Across
1. This is another word for large.
3. This is where the three bears lived.
5. Goldilocks sat in one.
7. This is another word for small.
8. This is not big and not small.

Down
1. This is where you sleep.
2. This is something Goldilocks ate.
4. This is the opposite of *cold.*
6. What you do when you are tired.

FS-32085 Crossword Puzzles

Name _____

Making Music

Read the clues. Write the music words in the puzzle.

drum
horn
violin
piano
guitar
note
music
listen
bells

Across
3. This instrument has black and white keys.
5. It is a musical sound.
6. You blow into this instrument.
7. Strike this instrument to make sounds.
9. Ring these to make sounds.

Down
1. You play the strings on this instrument with a bow.
2. People do this when they hear music.
4. An electric one is used for rock and roll.
8. It is another word for beautiful sounds.

Moving to Music

Read the clues. Write the movement words in the crossword puzzle.

stretch
move
dance
leap
glide
step
skip
whirl
pose

Across

3. This is another word for walk.
6. You turn fast when you do this.
7. It is a jump.
8. You do this when you move to music.

Down

1. You do this when you go from one place to another.
2. Reach out and make your body fill more space.
3. You do this when you move with little leaps.
4. You do this when you stand very still.
5. This means moving smoothly.

FS-32085 Crossword Puzzles

Fun in Art Class

Read the clues. Write the art words in the crossword puzzle.

paintbrush
color
paper
clay
glue
paints
chalk
scissors
markers

Across

2. Use this to make paper stick together.
5. Remember to put the caps back on these.
7. Make a pot with this.
8. Use your brushes with these.
9. Draw a picture on this.

Down

1. Purple is one.
3. Use this to spread paint on paper.
4. Make sidewalk drawings with this.
6. Use this to cut scraps for a picture.

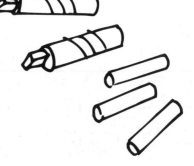

Our Family

Read the clues. Write the family words in the puzzle.

family
love
mother
father
sister
brother
grandmother
grandfather

Across

3. This is a boy in your family.
6. These are the people who love and take care of you.
7. This man is your parent.
8. A family gives this to each other.

Down

1. This woman is the mother of your mother or father.
2. This man is the father of your mother or father.
4. This woman is your parent.
5. This is a girl in your family.

Name _____

Going Places

Read the clues. Write the transportation words in the puzzle.

airplane
train
bike
bus
car
truck
boat
horse
balloon

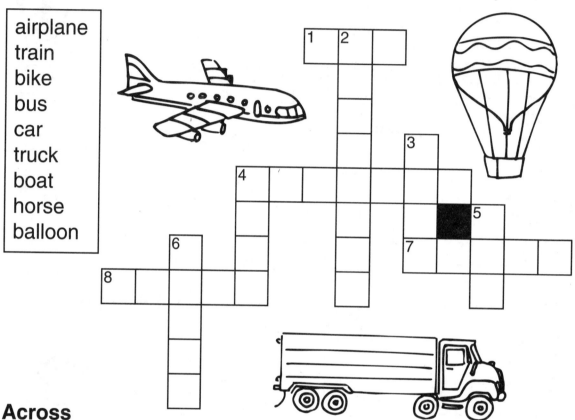

Across
1. It is an automobile.
4. Hot air makes it rise into the sky.
7. This can carry heavy loads on the road.
8. It has a saddle.

Down
2. This flies people from city to city.
3. This carries people and big loads on water.
4. It has two wheels and pedals.
5. This takes many people around the city.
6. It runs on tracks.

FS-32085 Crossword Puzzles

Around the City

Read the clues. Write the place names in the puzzle.

library
theater
park
museum
bank
drugstore
restaurant
school

Across
3. You can borrow books here.
4. Teachers help children learn here.
7. You can get something to eat here.
8. This is where you can go to play or ride a bike.

Down
1. Your mother or father can get medicine here.
2. This building has things about science, antiques, or art.
5. This is where you can see a movie.
6. This is a place where people keep money.

FS-32085 Crossword Puzzles

At School

Read the clues. Write the school words in the puzzle.

teacher
children
books
computer
desk
read
write
learn

Across

1. This is a machine that helps you learn.
4. You do this with a pencil or a computer.
5. This is where you can work in school.
7. This is a person who helps you learn.

Down

1. These are young people who go to school.
2. This is what you do with a book.
3. These have words and pictures in them.
6. This means *to find out about things.*

At a Powwow

Read the clues. Write the powwow words in the puzzle.

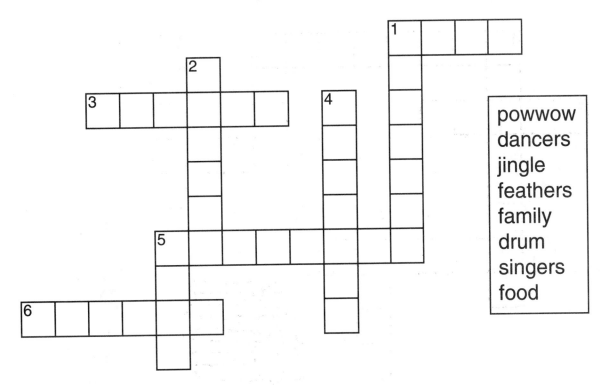

powwow
dancers
jingle
feathers
family
drum
singers
food

Across
1. You can hear this instrument at a powwow.
3. You might go to a powwow with these people.
5. Dancers wear them on their clothes.
6. You can see Native American dances there.

Down
1. They dance to the drum beat.
2. Some dancers wear bells that do this.
4. The people who sing are called this.
5. There is lots of this to eat at a powwow.

Around the World

Read the clues. Write the geography words in the puzzle.

map
north
south
globe
water
land
ball
equator
world

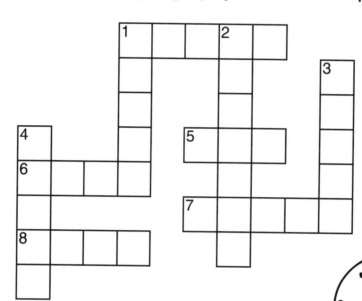

Across

1. It is blue on a globe.
5. It is a drawing of land and water on Earth.
6. It is green on a globe.
7. The direction moving toward the bottom of the globe.
8. This is the shape of a globe.

Down

1. A globe is a map of this.
2. It is an imaginary line around the middle of Earth.
3. The direction moving toward the top of the globe.
4. It is a model of Earth that is shaped like a ball.

Animal Homes

Read the clues. Write the animal homes in the puzzle.

web
tree
nest
lodge
hive
hill
shell
pond

Across

3. This is where bees make their honey.
4. This is a home for a clam.
6. Fish and frogs live here.
7. A bird makes this home.

Down

1. Ants build one to live in.
2. This is where a spider lives.
5. A beaver builds a dam near this home.
8. A hole in this makes a good home for a squirrel.

FS-32085 Crossword Puzzles

Winter

Read the clues. Write the winter words in the puzzle.

snowman
skis
ice
sleep
blizzard
indoors
shovel
bare
sled

Across
1. This is what some animals do in winter.
2. Use this to take the snow off of sidewalks.
3. This is where to stay warm in a snowstorm.
6. It is a snowstorm.

Down
1. You can build one in the snow.
2. Wear two of them on your feet.
4. Ride this down a snowy hill.
5. This is how the trees look in winter.
7. This is water that has frozen.

Spring

Read the clues. Write the spring words in the puzzle.

buds
warmer
flowers
caterpillar
windy
rainy
kite
outdoors

Across
2. It is the opposite of *colder*.
3. These bloom in the spring.
6. You can fly one outdoors in the spring.
7. Trees have these in the spring.
8. Take your umbrella on days like this.

Down
1. This is busy eating new leaves in spring.
4. It's fun to play here.
5. This is a good day to fly a kite.

Name _____

Summer

Read the clues. Write the summer words in the puzzle.

green
birds
butterflies
bees
hot
sunny
swim
picnic

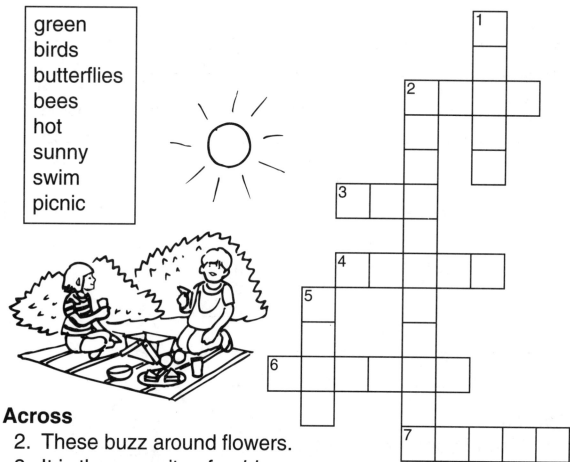

Across
2. These buzz around flowers.
3. It is the opposite of *cold*.
4. You might hear them chirp and sing.
6. Bring your lunch outside for this.
7. This kind of day is good for playing outside.

Down
1. Leaves and grass are this color.
2. They flutter their colorful wings.
5. This feels good to do on a hot summer day.

Name _____

Fall

Read the clues. Write the fall words in the crossword puzzle.

leaves
pumpkin
apples
moon
yellow
squirrels
geese
rake

Across
3. They gather nuts.
5. Use this to gather fallen leaves.
6. These change color in the fall.
8. This looks big and bright in the sky.

Down
1. Pick a big, orange one.
2. They fly south in the fall.
4. Leaves turn red, brown, and this color.
7. Pick a basket of red, ripe ones.

FS-32085 Crossword Puzzles

Name _____

The Calendar

Read the clues. Write the calendar words in the crossword puzzle.

days
week
month
year
calendar
holiday
birthday
time

Across

2. It is a day for celebrating instead of working.
3. It can be measured in days, weeks, months, and years.
4. It can have 28 to 31 days.
6. You can hang it on a wall to keep track of the days.
8. This has twelve months.

Down

1. This is the day you were born.
5. It has seven days.
7. A year has 365 of these.

Bird-watching

Read the clues. Write the bird words in the crossword puzzle.

feathers
nest
egg
fly
flock
birdhouse
wings
hatched
sing

Across

2. Birds flap their wings to do this.
3. It is where a mother bird lays eggs.
5. What a baby bird that comes out of its egg has done.
6. Many birds do this by making chirping sounds.
8. You can make one for a bird family.

Down

1. Birds have these on their bodies.
2. This is a group of birds.
4. This is what a mother bird lays.
7. A bird has two of these for flying.

Every Day Is Earth Day

Read the clues. Write the Earth words in the crossword puzzle.

paper
plant
recycle
litter
care
reuse
clean
walk

Across

2. This is made from trees.
5. This means *to watch over and protect.*
6. This is trash thrown on the ground.
8. This is the opposite of *polluted.*

Down

1. When people do this, it saves gas.
3. Make cans and bottles into new ones.
4. Do this to a tree.
7. This means *to use something again instead of throwing it away.*

FS-32085 Crossword Puzzles

Name _____

Good Manners

Read the clues. Write the words about manners in the crossword puzzle.

please
polite
loud
turns
cover
behave
thanks
bad
feelings

Across
1. Someone with good manners is called this.
3. This is what you should do to a sneeze.
5. Remember that other people have these.
6. If someone does something for you, tell them this.
7. When you ask for something, say this.
9. This is the kind of manners you don't want.

Down
2. When you play with others, everyone should take these.
4. Using good manners are how people do this.
8. This kind of noise may bother people.

© Frank Schaffer Publications, Inc. FS-32085 Crossword Puzzles

Math Fun

Read the clues. Write the math words in the puzzle.

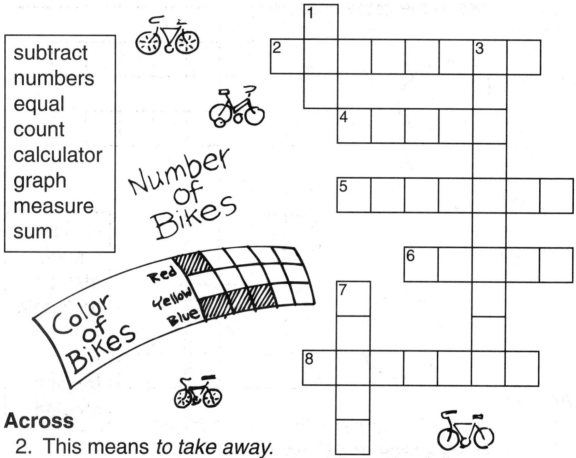

subtract
numbers
equal
count
calculator
graph
measure
sum

Number of Bikes

Color of Bikes

Red
Yellow
Blue

Across

2. This means *to take away.*
4. Things that are the same amount are this.
5. You can do this with a ruler.
6. It is a picture that shows math information.
8. These are words or marks that tell how many.

Down

1. It is the answer when you add numbers.
3. It is a tool that does math.
7. Say the numbers in order.

Shapes

Read the clues. Write the shape words in the crossword puzzle.

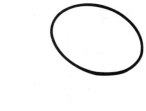

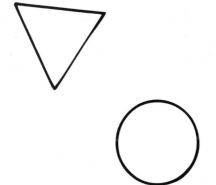

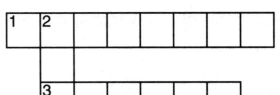

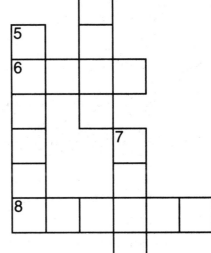

Word Box
- circle
- square
- triangle
- rectangle
- oval
- half
- fraction
- shapes

Across

1. It is a part of a whole.
3. This is the shape of the moon.
4. It is a shape with three sides.
6. It is one of two equal parts.
8. It is a rectangle that has four equal sides.

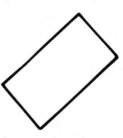

Down

2. This is a shape with four sides.
5. It is another name for circles, triangles, and squares.
7. This is the shape of an egg.

FS-32085 Crossword Puzzles

Counting Money

Read the clues. Write the money words in the puzzle.

dollar
cent
quarter
nickel
dime
penny
buy
hundred
coin

Across

3. It is worth ten cents.
4. It is worth five cents.
6. It is worth twenty-five cents.
8. It is worth one cent.

Down

1. It is another name for a penny.
2. It is another name for a dime, nickel, or penny.
3. It equals one hundred cents.
5. This is how many pennies there are in a dollar.
7. You can save your money or you can do this.

Name _____

Computer Talk

Read the clues. Write the computer words in the puzzle.

Across
   3. Look here to see words or pictures.
   5. A computer in school helps you do this.
   8. These are on computer keys.

Down
   1. This machine will put words on paper.
   2. Press these on a computer to tell it what to do.
   4. This has many keys on it.
   6. Some computers have this kind of clicker.
   7. This means to make up stories or poems.

learn
keyboard
screen
keys
letters
write
printer
mouse

FS-32085 Crossword Puzzles

Name _____

We Love Fruit

Read the clues. Write the names of fruits in the puzzle.

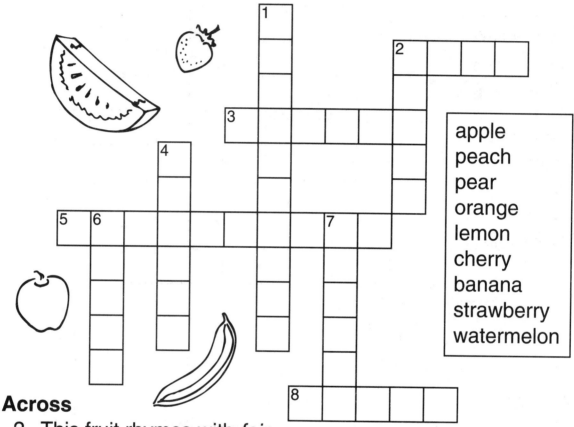

apple
peach
pear
orange
lemon
cherry
banana
strawberry
watermelon

Across

2. This fruit rhymes with *fair*.
3. It is a yellow fruit you can slice on your cereal.
5. It is a large green fruit that is red inside.
8. You can make lemonade with this fruit.

Down

1. This small red fruit goes with shortcake.
2. It is a fruit with a fuzzy skin.
4. This small red fruit grows on trees and has a pit.
6. You might eat this red fruit cooked in a pie.
7. This fruit and its color have the same name.

FS-32085 Crossword Puzzles

In the Garden

Read the clues. Write the garden words in the puzzle.

scarecrow
dig
rows
plant
seeds
water
hoe
weeds
ladybugs

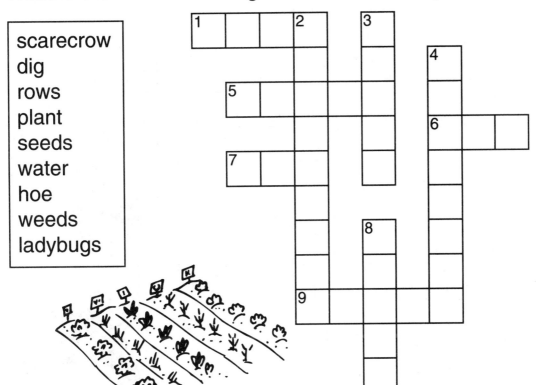

Across
1. These are lines of vegetables in a garden.
5. This is what you do when you put seeds in soil.
6. This is how you make a hole in the ground.
7. It is a tool with a long handle.
9. You don't want these to grow in your garden.

Down
2. Stand this in the garden to keep away birds.
3. Plants need this to grow.
4. These insects will help your garden.
8. These start out small, but grow into big plants.

Playground Fun

Read the clues. Write the playground words in the puzzle.

tag
slide
swing
climb
friends
recess
rope
hopscotch
sand

Across
5. It is a break from schoolwork.
6. This is how you go up a slide.
7. In this game, you run and touch someone.
8. If it's slippery, you'll go down fast.

Down
1. You can jump it.
2. To play this game, draw it on a sidewalk.
3. They are people you like to play with.
4. Sit on this and pump your legs to move.
8. You can dig in this and make roads.

Sports

Read the clues. Write the sports words in the crossword puzzle.

baseball
run
kart
horseback
skating
bicycle
soccer
gymnastics

Across
2. This kind of riding is done on a horse.
5. When you do this, your legs carry you fast.
7. This has two wheels, pedals, and a seat.
8. A sport that has exercises to make strong muscles.

Down
1. This is played with a bat and ball.
3. This is a little racing car.
4. Hockey players are good at this.
6. You can't use your hands, but you can kick this ball.

Name _____

In the Snow

Read the clues. Write the snow words in the crossword puzzle.

snowball
sled
snowman
angel
fort
tracks
skate
skis

Across

2. He has eyes of coal and a carrot nose.
3. Put these on your feet and go down the hill.
4. A pile of snow that you can hide behind.
5. You do this on ice.
6. Move your arms in the snow to make its wings.

Down

1. Your feet make these in the snow.
2. Throw it at a tree, but not at a person.
3. Let your friend sit on it while you pull.

FS-32085 Crossword Puzzles

Camping

Read the clues. Write the camping words in the puzzle.

tent
raccoon
campfire
flashlight
woods
owl
log
trail
sing

Across

3. This animal has a ringed tail and comes out at night.
5. You can use it to make a campfire.
7. People like to do this around the campfire.
8. Take this with you so you can see in the dark.

Down

1. It is a path in the woods.
2. It is another name for forest.
4. This is good for roasting marshmallows over.
6. You can hear this bird hooting at night.
9. It is a place to sleep when you are camping.

FS-32085 Crossword Puzzles

The Circus

Read the clues. Write the circus words in the puzzle.

clown
acrobat
trapeze
lion
juggler
tent
ringmaster
horseback
wire

Across

2. This person can swing on a trapeze.
5. This person is in charge of the circus ring.
6. This person wears a funny nose and a painted smile.
7. It is like a swing.
8. An acrobat can walk on one high up in the air.

Down

1. Acrobats stand while riding like this.
3. This person can do tricks with balls.
4. A trainer works with this animal.
7. The circus is inside of this.

FS-32085 Crossword Puzzles

Answer Key

Page 1

Color Words

Name _____

Write the color of the fruit or vegetable to complete the puzzle.

Word Box
red   orange
yellow   green
blue   purple

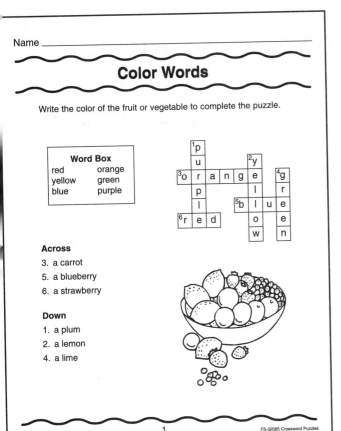

Crossword grid:
- ¹p u p l
- ²y
- ³o r a n g e
- ⁴g r e e n
- ⁵b l u e
- ⁶r e d
- y e l l o w

Across
3. a carrot
5. a blueberry
6. a strawberry

Down
1. a plum
2. a lemon
4. a lime

1   FS-32085 Crossword Puzzles

Page 2

How Many Toys?

Name _____

Count. Write the number word for each clue.

Word Box
one
two
three
four
five
six
seven
eight
nine
ten

Across
2.
3.
4.
6.
7.

Crossword grid:
- ¹o n e
- ²t h r e e
- t w
- ³f o u r
- i
- v
- ⁴e i g h ⁵t
- e
- ⁶s i x
- ⁷n i n e
- e v e n

Down
1.
2.
3.
5.
6.

2   FS-32085 Crossword Puzzles

Page 3

Counting Clothes

Name _____

Count. Write the number word for each clue.

Across
2.
4.

Down
1.
2.
3.

Crossword grid:
- ¹t h i r t e e n
- ²f o u r t e ³e n
- i e
- f l
- t e
- ⁴t w e l v e
- e n

Word Box
eleven
twelve
thirteen
fourteen
fifteen

3   FS-32085 Crossword Puzzles

Page 4

Measurement

Name _____

Read each sentence and use the words in the Work Box to complete the puzzle.

Crossword grid:
- ¹i
- ²p i n t
- o c
- ³y u h
- ⁴g a l ⁵l o n
- r i d
- d t
- s e
- r

Word Box
gallon   pound
liter   yards
inch   pint

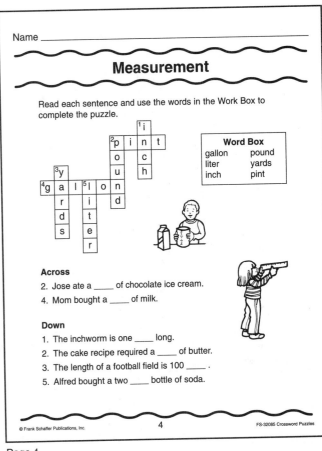

Across
2. Jose ate a _____ of chocolate ice cream.
4. Mom bought a _____ of milk.

Down
1. The inchworm is one _____ long.
2. The cake recipe required a _____ of butter.
3. The length of a football field is 100 _____ .
5. Alfred bought a two _____ bottle of soda.

4   FS-32085 Crossword Puzzles

FS-32085 Crossword Puzzles

Answer Key

At the Pet Shop

Name _____

Read the clues and use the words in the Word Box to complete the puzzle.

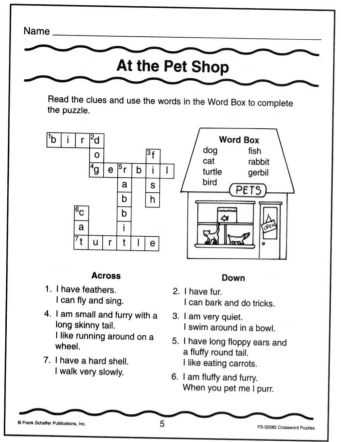

Word Box

dog	fish
cat	rabbit
turtle	gerbil
bird	

PETS

Across

1. I have feathers.
   I can fly and sing.
4. I am small and furry with a long skinny tail.
   I like running around on a wheel.
7. I have a hard shell.
   I walk very slowly.

Down

2. I have fur.
   I can bark and do tricks.
3. I am very quiet.
   I swim around in a bowl.
5. I have long floppy ears and a fluffy round tail.
   I like eating carrots.
6. I am fluffy and furry.
   When you pet me I purr.

5

FS-32085 Crossword Puzzles

Page 5

Baby Animals

Name _____

Find the baby animal for each adult animal to complete the puzzle.

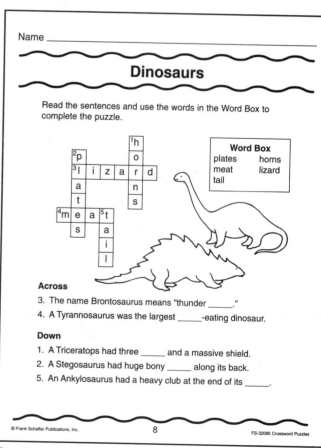

Word Box

chick	fawn
puppy	kitten
foal	tadpole
duckling	calf

Across

3. cow
5. cat
7. dog
8. duck

Down

1. horse
2. hen
4. deer
6. frog

6

FS-32085 Crossword Puzzles

Page 6

Animal Coverings

Name _____

Find the type of covering for each animal to complete the puzzle.

Word Box

shell	quills
fur	feathers
skin	scales

Across

1. snow hare
3. elephant
5. goldfish

Down

1. swan
2. porcupine
3. turtle

7

FS-32085 Crossword Puzzles

Page 7

Dinosaurs

Name _____

Read the sentences and use the words in the Word Box to complete the puzzle.

Word Box

plates	horns
meat	lizard
tail	

Across

3. The name Brontosaurus means "thunder _____."
4. A Tyrannosaurus was the largest _____-eating dinosaur.

Down

1. A Triceratops had three _____ and a massive shield.
2. A Stegosaurus had huge bony _____ along its back.
5. An Ankylosaurus had a heavy club at the end of its _____.

8

FS-32085 Crossword Puzzles

Page 8

FS-32085 Crossword Puzzles

Answer Key

Mammals

Name _____

Read the clues and use the words in the Word Box to complete the puzzle.

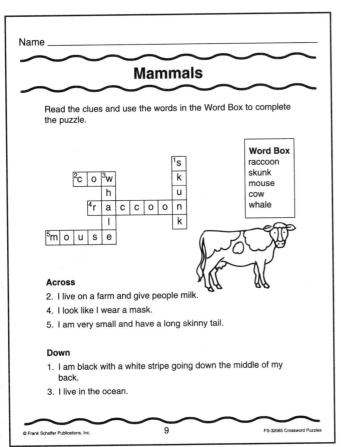

Word Box
raccoon
skunk
mouse
cow
whale

Across

2. I live on a farm and give people milk.
4. I look like I wear a mask.
5. I am very small and have a long skinny tail.

Down

1. I am black with a white stripe going down the middle of my back.
3. I live in the ocean.

9   FS-32085 Crossword Puzzles

Page 9

Amphibians and Reptiles

Name _____

Read the sentences and use the words in the Word Box to complete the puzzle.

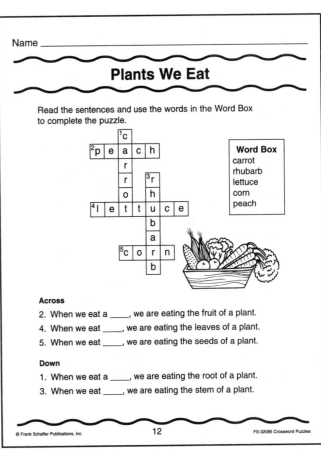

Word Box
amphibian
reptile
turtle
crocodile
frog

Across

2. A _____ is a reptile that has a shell and pulls its head, legs, and tail into the shell for protection.
3. An _____ is a cold-blooded animal that has scaleless skin and lives part of its life in water.
5. A _____ is a reptile that has a long snout.

Down

1. A _____ is a cold-blooded animal that has dry, scaly skin.
4. A _____ is an amphibian that has four legs and no tail.

10   FS-32085 Crossword Puzzles

Page 10

Parts of a Plant

Name _____

Read the clues and use the words in the Word Box to complete the puzzle.

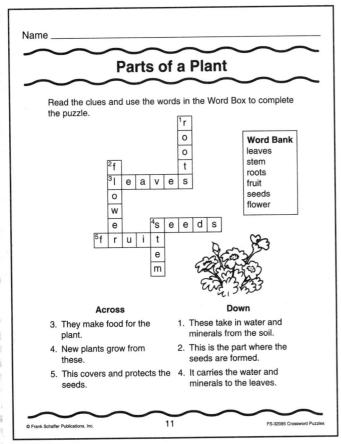

Word Bank
leaves
stem
roots
fruit
seeds
flower

Across

3. They make food for the plant.
4. New plants grow from these.
5. This covers and protects the seeds.

Down

1. These take in water and minerals from the soil.
2. This is the part where the seeds are formed.
4. It carries the water and minerals to the leaves.

11   FS-32085 Crossword Puzzles

Page 11

Plants We Eat

Name _____

Read the sentences and use the words in the Word Box to complete the puzzle.

Word Box
carrot
rhubarb
lettuce
corn
peach

Across

2. When we eat a _____, we are eating the fruit of a plant.
4. When we eat _____, we are eating the leaves of a plant.
5. When we eat _____, we are eating the seeds of a plant.

Down

1. When we eat a _____, we are eating the root of a plant.
3. When we eat _____, we are eating the stem of a plant.

12   FS-32085 Crossword Puzzles

Page 12

FS-32085 Crossword Puzzles

Answer Key

Living Things

Read the clues and use the words in the tree to complete the puzzle.

Word tree:
girl
flower
tree
eagle
fish
elephant

Crossword:
- ¹g i r ²e a g l e
- ³f l o w e r
- fish / elephant / tree

Across

2. I can fly.

3. I am a plant. I have petals and smell pretty.

4. I have a trunk, leaves, and branches.

Down

1. I am a person.

2. I am a large gray animal with a long trunk and big, floppy ears.

3. I live in the water and can swim.

© Frank Schaffer Publications, Inc.   13   FS-32085 Crossword Puzzles

Page 13

Nonliving Things

Read the sentences and use the words in the Word Box to complete the puzzle.

Word Box
chair
ball
telephone
bicycle
swing
sweater

Crossword:
- ¹b
- ²s w i n g
- ³t e l e p h o n e
- ⁴b
- ⁵c h a i r

Across

2. A _____ is something you play on.

3. A _____ is something you call people on to talk to them.

5. A _____ is something that has four legs and you sit on it.

Down

1. A _____ is something you ride on that has two wheels.

2. A _____ is something you wear to keep you warm.

4. A _____ is something you can throw and catch.

© Frank Schaffer Publications, Inc.   14   FS-32085 Crossword Puzzles

Page 14

Fishes

Read the sentences and use the words in the Word Box to complete the puzzle.

Word Box
colors   ocean
lakes   fins
mouths   gills

Crossword:
- ¹o ²c e a n
- ³m o u t h s
- ⁴g i ⁵l l s
- ⁶f i n s

Across

1. Saltwater fish live in the _____.

3. Fish open and close their _____ as they swim to get air from the water.

4. The water comes out of their _____.

6. Fish have tails and _____.

Down

2. Fish are many different sizes, shapes, and _____.

5. Freshwater fish live in ponds, rivers, or _____.

© Frank Schaffer Publications, Inc.   15   FS-32085 Crossword Puzzles

Page 15

Forest Life

Read the sentences and use the words in the Word Box to complete the puzzle.

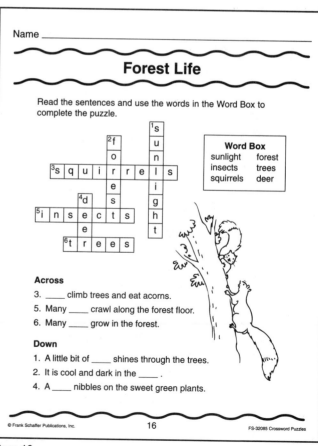

Word Box
sunlight   forest
insects   trees
squirrels   deer

Crossword:
- ¹s
- ²f
- ³s q u i r r e l s
- ⁴d
- ⁵i n s e c t s
- ⁶t r e e s

Across

3. _____ climb trees and eat acorns.

5. Many _____ crawl along the forest floor.

6. Many _____ grow in the forest.

Down

1. A little bit of _____ shines through the trees.

2. It is cool and dark in the _____.

4. A _____ nibbles on the sweet green plants.

© Frank Schaffer Publications, Inc.   16   FS-32085 Crossword Puzzles

Page 16

Answer Key

Desert Life

Name _____

Read the sentences and use the words in the Word Box to complete the puzzle.

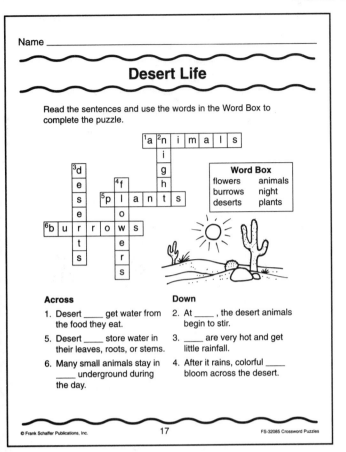

Word Box

flowers	animals
burrows	night
deserts	plants

Across answers: ¹aⁿimals, ⁵plants, ⁶burrows
Down answers: night, foowers, deserts

Across

1. Desert ____ get water from the food they eat.
5. Desert ____ store water in their leaves, roots, or stems.
6. Many small animals stay in ____ underground during the day.

Down

2. At ____ , the desert animals begin to stir.
3. ____ are very hot and get little rainfall.
4. After it rains, colorful ____ bloom across the desert.

Page 17

At the Pond

Name _____

Read the sentences and use the words in the Word Box to complete the puzzle.

Word Box

cattails	fish
lily pad	willow
turtle	pond

Answers: ¹turtle, ²willow, ³cattails, ⁴lily pad, ⁵pond, ⁶fish

Across

4. A bullfrog sits on a ____ and croaks a loud song.
5. A family of ducks waddle into the ____ for a swim.
6. A raccoon tries to catch a ____ as it swims by.

Down

1. A ____ sits on a rock in the morning sun.
2. The weeping ____ gives shade to the animals.
3. Birds fly over the many ____ sticking out of the water.

Page 18

Land and Water

Name _____

Read the clues and use the words in the Word Box to complete the puzzle.

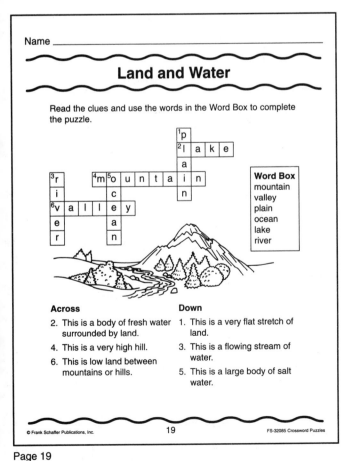

Word Box

mountain
valley
plain
ocean
lake
river

Answers: ¹plain, ²lake, ³river, ⁴mountain, ⁵ocean, ⁶valley

Across

2. This is a body of fresh water surrounded by land.
4. This is a very high hill.
6. This is low land between mountains or hills.

Down

1. This is a very flat stretch of land.
3. This is a flowing stream of water.
5. This is a large body of salt water.

Page 19

Magnets

Name _____

Read the sentences and use the words in the Word Box to complete the puzzle.

Word Box

bar
paper clip
poles
eraser
horseshoe
ring

Answers: ¹horseshoe, ²ring, ³brush, ⁴paper clip, ⁵poles, ⁶eraser

Across

2. This is a ____ magnet.
4. A magnet will attract a ____ .
6. A magnet will not attract an ____ .

Down

1. This is a ____ magnet.
3. This is a ____ magnet.
5. The ____ are at the ends of a magnet.

Page 20

Answer Key

Solids, Liquids, Gases

Read the sentences and use the words in the Word Box to complete the puzzle.

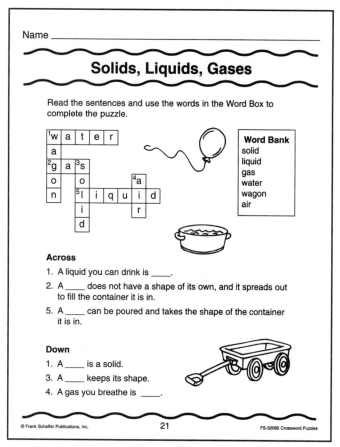

Word Bank
solid
liquid
gas
water
wagon
air

Across

1. A liquid you can drink is ____.

2. A ____ does not have a shape of its own, and it spreads out to fill the container it is in.

5. A ____ can be poured and takes the shape of the container it is in.

Down

1. A ____ is a solid.

3. A ____ keeps its shape.

4. A gas you breathe is ____.

© Frank Schaffer Publications, Inc.   21   FS-32085 Crossword Puzzles

Page 21

Being a Friend

Read the sentences and use the words in the Word Box to complete the puzzle.

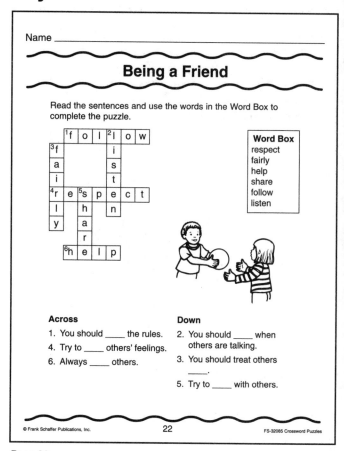

Word Box
respect
fairly
help
share
follow
listen

Across

1. You should ____ the rules.

4. Try to ____ others' feelings.

6. Always ____ others.

Down

2. You should ____ when others are talking.

3. You should treat others ____.

5. Try to ____ with others.

© Frank Schaffer Publications, Inc.   22   FS-32085 Crossword Puzzles

Page 22

Feelings

Look at the picture clues and use the words in the Word Box to complete the puzzle.

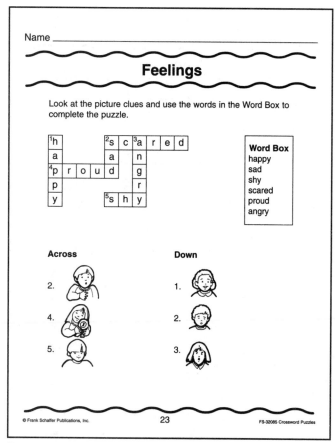

Word Box
happy
sad
shy
scared
proud
angry

Across

2.

4.

5.

Down

1.

2.

3.

© Frank Schaffer Publications, Inc.   23   FS-32085 Crossword Puzzles

Page 23

Healthy Foods

Read the sentences and use the words in the Word Box to complete the puzzle.

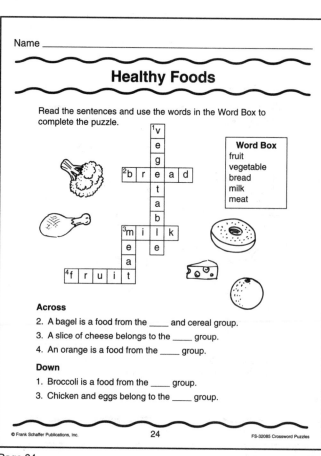

Word Box
fruit
vegetable
bread
milk
meat

Across

2. A bagel is a food from the ____ and cereal group.

3. A slice of cheese belongs to the ____ group.

4. An orange is a food from the ____ group.

Down

1. Broccoli is a food from the ____ group.

3. Chicken and eggs belong to the ____ group.

© Frank Schaffer Publications, Inc.   24   FS-32085 Crossword Puzzles

Page 24

Answer Key

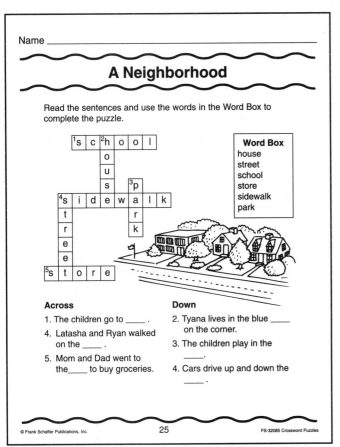

A Neighborhood

Read the sentences and use the words in the Word Box to complete the puzzle.

Word Box
house
street
school
store
sidewalk
park

Across
1. The children go to ____ .
4. Latasha and Ryan walked on the ____ .
5. Mom and Dad went to the ____ to buy groceries.

Down
2. Tyana lives in the blue ____ on the corner.
3. The children play in the ____.
4. Cars drive up and down the ____ .

Page 25

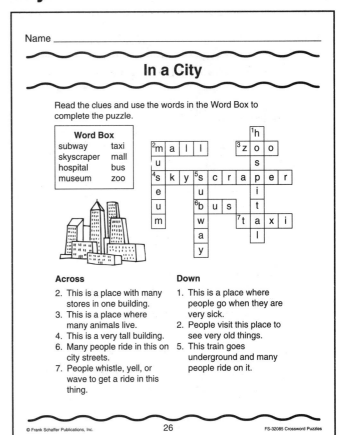

In a City

Read the clues and use the words in the Word Box to complete the puzzle.

Word Box
subway   taxi
skyscraper   mall
hospital   bus
museum   zoo

Across
2. This is a place with many stores in one building.
3. This is a place where many animals live.
4. This is a very tall building.
6. Many people ride in this on city streets.
7. People whistle, yell, or wave to get a ride in this thing.

Down
1. This is a place where people go when they are very sick.
2. People visit this place to see very old things.
5. This train goes underground and many people ride on it.

Page 26

Safety

Read the clues and use the words in the Word Box to complete the puzzle

Word Box
seat belt
helmet
life jacket
stop sign
traffic light

Across
4. I tell cars when to stop and go.
5. I help you keep afloat when you are in the water.

Down
1. I am red with white letters. I sit on a post.
2. You wear me on your head when you ride a bike.
3. You wear me when you ride in a car.

Page 27

Fire Safety

Read the sentences and use the words in the Word Box to complete the puzzle.

Word Box
breathe   shout
opening   roll
call   calm

Across
2. Feel the door first before ____ it.
3. Stay low, close to the floor, to ____ the cleaner air.
6. You should ____ 9-1-1 immediately.

Down
1. You can ____ loudly to let people know there's a fire.
4. Stop, drop, and ____ if your clothing is on fire.
5. Stay ____.

Page 28

Answer Key

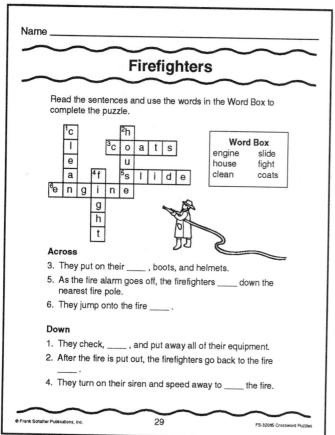

Firefighters

Read the sentences and use the words in the Word Box to complete the puzzle.

Word Box
engine   slide
house   fight
clean   coats

Across

3. They put on their ____ , boots, and helmets.
5. As the fire alarm goes off, the firefighters ____ down the nearest fire pole.
6. They jump onto the fire ____ .

Down

1. They check, ____ , and put away all of their equipment.
2. After the fire is put out, the firefighters go back to the fire ____ .
4. They turn on their siren and speed away to ____ the fire.

© Frank Schaffer Publications, Inc.   29   FS-32085 Crossword Puzzles

Page 29

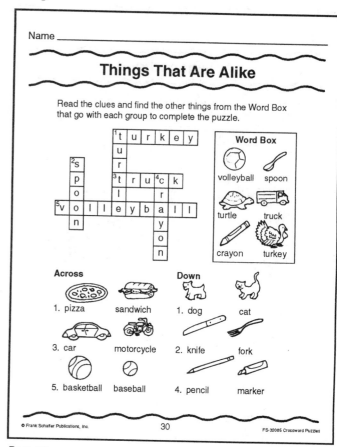

Things That Are Alike

Read the clues and find the other things from the Word Box that go with each group to complete the puzzle.

Word Box
volleyball   spoon
turtle   truck
crayon   turkey

Across

1. pizza   sandwich
3. car   motorcycle
5. basketball   baseball

Down

1. dog   cat
2. knife   fork
4. pencil   marker

© Frank Schaffer Publications, Inc.   30   FS-32085 Crossword Puzzles

Page 30

Rhyming Puzzle

Read each clue and find the rhyming word for the word in **dark print** to complete the puzzle.

Word Box
blocks   fair
plane   swing
flower   moon
bee   name

Across

2. It's going to **rain**. I'm flying in a ____ .
4. You eat with a **spoon**. There is a full ____ .
5. I climbed a **tree**. I was stung by a ____ .
6. There's a chance of a rain **shower**. Sue has a red ____ .

Down

1. Maria has a **ring**. I played on the ____ .
3. Did you play a **game**. What is your ____ ?
5. Sue lost her **socks**. Mike played with the ____ .
6. I'll cut my **hair**. Ben saw a pig at the county ____ .

© Frank Schaffer Publications, Inc.   31   FS-32085 Crossword Puzzles

Page 31

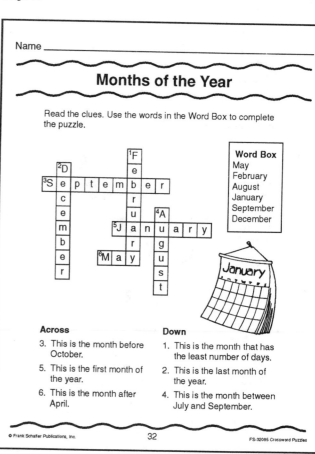

Months of the Year

Read the clues. Use the words in the Word Box to complete the puzzle.

Word Box
May
February
August
January
September
December

Across

3. This is the month before October.
5. This is the first month of the year.
6. This is the month after April.

Down

1. This is the month that has the least number of days.
2. This is the last month of the year.
4. This is the month between July and September.

© Frank Schaffer Publications, Inc.   32   FS-32085 Crossword Puzzles

Page 32

FS-32085 Crossword Puzzles

Answer Key

Animal Alphabet

Write each group of words in ABC order.
Write the words in the puzzle.

```
              ¹f
   ²g i r a f f e
              r
              r
        ³g    e
   ⁴h i p p o p o t a ⁵m u s
     o   r           o
     r   i           n
     s   l           k
   ⁶s e a l          ⁷z e b r a
         a
```

Across

zebra   seal
hippopotamus giraffe

Down

monkey   gorilla
horse   ferret

2. giraffe
4. hippopotamus
6. seal
7. zebra

1. ferret
3. gorilla
4. horse
5. monkey

33

© Frank Schaffer Publications, Inc.   FS-32085 Crossword Puzzles

Page 33

Find the Nouns

Nouns are words that name a person, place, or thing.
Read each clue and find the noun to complete the puzzle.

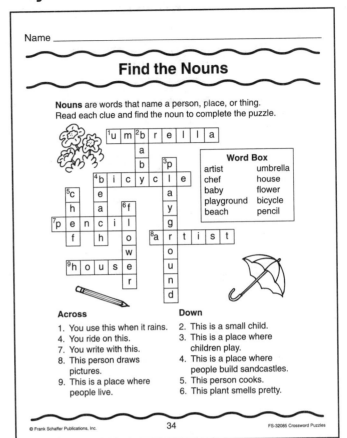

```
        ¹u m ²b r e l l a
              a
              b       ³p
         ⁴b i c y c l e
   ⁵c    e         a
   h     a    ⁶f    y
   ⁷p e n c i l    g
   f     h    o    ⁸a r t i s t
   w         w
   ⁹h o u s e r
```

Word Box

artist   umbrella
chef   house
baby   flower
playground bicycle
beach   pencil

Across

1. You use this when it rains.
4. You ride on this.
7. You write with this.
8. This person draws
   pictures.
9. This is a place where
   people live.

Down

2. This is a small child.
3. This is a place where
   children play.
4. This is a place where
   people build sandcastles.
5. This person cooks.
6. This plant smells pretty.

34

© Frank Schaffer Publications, Inc.   FS-32085 Crossword Puzzles

Page 34

Lights, Camera, Action

A **verb** is an action word. It tells what the noun in the
sentence does or is doing. Read each sentence and find the
verb to complete the puzzle.

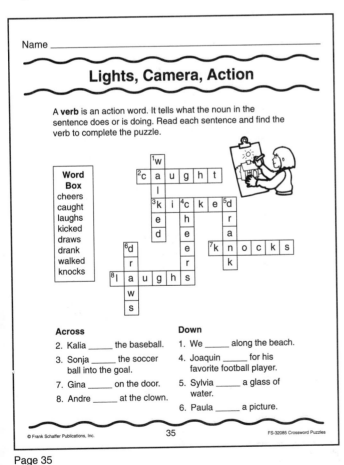

**Word
Box**

cheers
caught
laughs
kicked
draws
drank
walked
knocks

```
        ¹w
   ²c a u g h t
        l
      ³k i ⁴c k e ⁵d
        e   h    r
        d   e    a
      ⁶d   e    ⁷k n o c k s
      r   r    k
   ⁸l a u g h s
      w
      s
```

Across

2. Kalia _____ the baseball.
3. Sonja _____ the soccer
   ball into the goal.
7. Gina _____ on the door.
8. Andre _____ at the clown.

Down

1. We _____ along the beach.
4. Joaquin _____ for his
   favorite football player.
5. Sylvia _____ a glass of
   water.
6. Paula _____ a picture.

35

© Frank Schaffer Publications, Inc.   FS-32085 Crossword Puzzles

Page 35

Adjective Puzzle

An **adjective** tells or describes more about the noun. Read
each clue and find the adjective that best describes the noun.

Word Box

beautiful juicy
young   soft
fluffy   salty
funny   thick

```
                        ¹f
        ²b e a u ³t i f u l
   ⁴s        h        u
   a      ⁵f i  ⁶s o f t
   l      ⁷j u i c y    f
   t      n    k       y
   ⁸y o u n g
         y
```

Across

2. _____ flower
6. _____ pillow
7. _____ orange
8. _____ child

Down

1. _____ kitten
3. _____ milk shake
4. _____ pickle
5. _____ clown

36

© Frank Schaffer Publications, Inc.   FS-32085 Crossword Puzzles

Page 36

© Frank Schaffer Publications, Inc.   FS-32085 Crossword Puzzles

Answer Key

Contraction Puzzle

A **contraction** is two words written as one with an apostrophe taking the place of the missing letters. Read each clue and find the words for the contraction in **dark print**.

Word Box
I am
she will
we have
he is
is not
they would
they are
they have

Across
3. **He's** having a party.
4. **They're** going to the movies.
6. **She'll** fix the car.
7. **We've** been swimming in the lake.

Down
1. **I'm** thirsty.
2. **They'd** like to be in the school play.
4. I think **they've** moved.
5. Bryan **isn't** tired.

Page 37

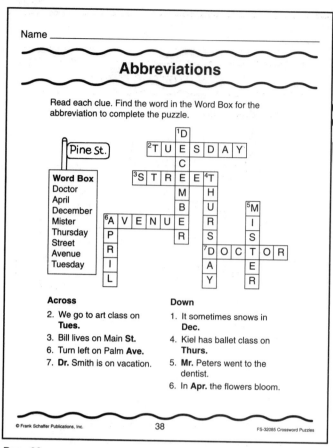

Abbreviations

Read each clue. Find the word in the Word Box for the abbreviation to complete the puzzle.

Pine St.

Word Box
Doctor
April
December
Mister
Thursday
Street
Avenue
Tuesday

Across
2. We go to art class on **Tues.**
3. Bill lives on Main **St.**
6. Turn left on Palm **Ave.**
7. **Dr.** Smith is on vacation.

Down
1. It sometimes snows in **Dec.**
4. Kiel has ballet class on **Thurs.**
5. **Mr.** Peters went to the dentist.
6. In **Apr.** the flowers bloom.

Page 38

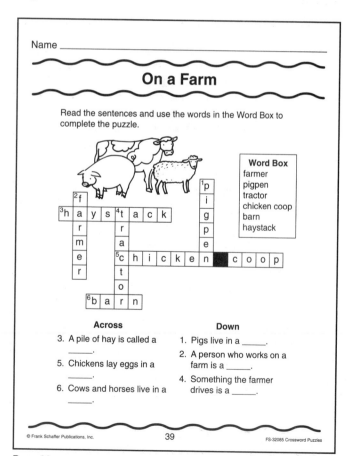

On a Farm

Read the sentences and use the words in the Word Box to complete the puzzle.

Word Box
farmer
pigpen
tractor
chicken coop
barn
haystack

Across
3. A pile of hay is called a _____.
5. Chickens lay eggs in a _____.
6. Cows and horses live in a _____.

Down
1. Pigs live in a _____.
2. A person who works on a farm is a _____.
4. Something the farmer drives is a _____.

Page 39

Animal Homes

Use the clues to complete the puzzle.

Word Box
spider   prairie dog   woodpecker
beaver   bear   honeybee

Across
4. My home is a burrow.
5. My home is a web.
6. My home is a den.

Down
1. My home is a hive.
2. My home is a lodge.
3. My home is a hole in a tree.

Page 40

Answer Key

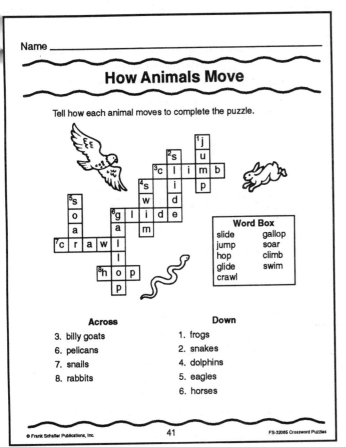

How Animals Move

Tell how each animal moves to complete the puzzle.

Word Box
slide   gallop
jump   soar
hop   climb
glide   swim
crawl

Across
3. billy goats
6. pelicans
7. snails
8. rabbits

Down
1. frogs
2. snakes
4. dolphins
5. eagles
6. horses

41   FS-32085 Crossword Puzzles

Page 41

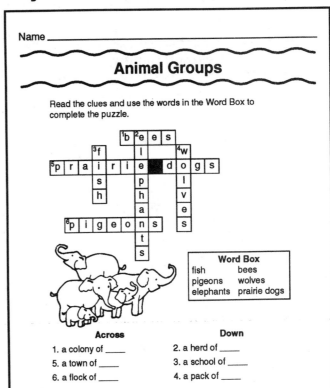

Animal Groups

Read the clues and use the words in the Word Box to complete the puzzle.

Word Box
fish   bees
pigeons   wolves
elephants   prairie dogs

Across
1. a colony of ____
5. a town of ____
6. a flock of ____

Down
2. a herd of ____
3. a school of ____
4. a pack of ____

42   FS-32085 Crossword Puzzles

Page 42

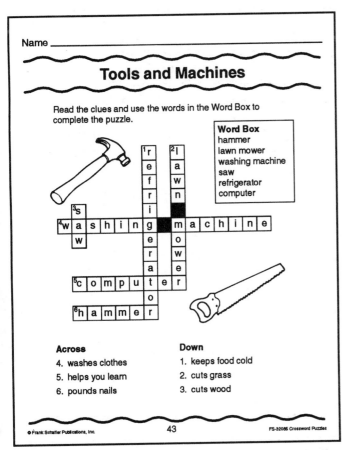

Tools and Machines

Read the clues and use the words in the Word Box to complete the puzzle.

Word Box
hammer
lawn mower
washing machine
saw
refrigerator
computer

Across
4. washes clothes
5. helps you learn
6. pounds nails

Down
1. keeps food cold
2. cuts grass
3. cuts wood

43   FS-32085 Crossword Puzzles

Page 43

At the Beach

Read the sentences and use the words in the Word Box to complete the puzzle.

Word Box
ocean
seashells
umbrella
sandcastle
shovel
beachball

Across
2. My family sat under the beach ____ and ate lunch.
4. At the beach, I built a ____ .
6. We saw dolphins swimming in the ____ .

Down
1. I took a walk along the shore to look for ____ .
3. My brother and I tossed the ____ .
5. I used my pail and ____ to build a sandcastle.

44   FS-32085 Crossword Puzzles

Page 44

FS-32085 Crossword Puzzles

Answer Key

Keeping Healthy

Name _____

Read the sentences and use the words in the Word Box to complete the puzzle.

Word Box
- exercise
- eat
- sleep
- brush
- safety rules
- bath
- comb

Across
2. Take a _____.
3. You should _____ your muscles.
6. Remember to _____ your teeth.
7. Always _____ healthy foods.

Down
1. Follow the _____ _____.
4. Brush or _____ your hair.
5. Get plenty of _____.

45
FS-32085 Crossword Puzzles

Page 45

Community Helpers

Name _____

Read the clues and use the words in the Word Box to complete the puzzle.

Word Box
- firefighter
- teacher
- police officer
- doctor
- mail carrier
- dentist

Across
2. I deliver packages to homes almost every day.
5. You come to me for help when you are lost.
6. I help you learn.

Down
1. I drive a long, red truck with ladders and hoses.
3. You visit me when your tooth hurts.
4. Sometimes you visit me when you are sick.

46
FS-32085 Crossword Puzzles

Page 46

People Who Work At Night

Name _____

Read the sentences and use the words in the Word Box to complete the puzzle.

Word Box
- baker
- reporter
- custodian
- waiter
- security guard
- paramedic

Across
2. A _____ writes news stories for newspapers.
5. A _____ makes fresh bread and rolls.
6. A _____ protects buildings.

Down
1. A _____ cleans offices and schools.
3. A _____ drives an ambulance and helps people when they are sick.
4. A _____ serves people food in a restaurant.

47
FS-32085 Crossword Puzzles

Page 47

Addition Fun

Name _____

Add. Write the number word for each answer in the puzzle.

Word Box
- one
- two
- three
- four
- five
- six
- seven
- eight
- nine
- ten

Across

a. $2 + 2$ c. $5 + 3$ e. $3 + 4$ g. $6 + 4$

Down

a. $3 + 2$ b. $2 + 1$ d. $0 + 1$ e. $4 + 2$ f. $7 + 2$ g. $1 + 1$

48
FS-32085 Crossword Puzzles

Page 48

FS-32085 Crossword Puzzles

Answer Key

Page 49

Name _____

Subtraction Fun

Subtract. Write the number word for each answer in the puzzle.

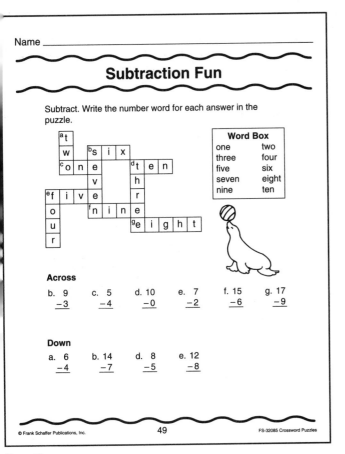

Word Box

one	two
three	four
five	six
seven	eight
nine	ten

Across

b. $9 - 3$ c. $5 - 4$ d. $10 - 0$ e. $7 - 2$ f. $15 - 6$ g. $17 - 9$

Down

a. $6 - 4$ b. $14 - 7$ d. $8 - 5$ e. $12 - 8$

© Frank Schaffer Publications, Inc.   49   FS-32085 Crossword Puzzles

Page 50

Name _____

Addition Puzzle

Solve each addition problem. Write the answers in the puzzle.

863	794
496	439
571	746
266	756
823	968

Across

b. $350 + 221$ d. $423 + 323$ f. $324 + 115$ i. $135 + 131$ j. $522 + 341$

Down

a. $522 + 234$ c. $652 + 142$ e. $375 + 121$ g. $644 + 324$ h. $202 + 621$

© Frank Schaffer Publications, Inc.   50   FS-32085 Crossword Puzzles

Page 51

Name _____

Subtraction Puzzle

Solve each addition problem. Write the answers in the puzzle.

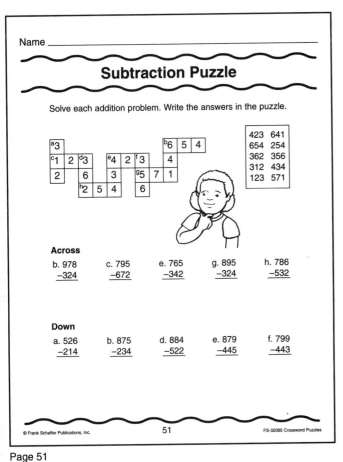

423	641
654	254
362	356
312	434
123	571

Across

b. $978 - 324$ c. $795 - 672$ e. $765 - 342$ g. $895 - 324$ h. $786 - 532$

Down

a. $526 - 214$ b. $875 - 234$ d. $884 - 522$ e. $879 - 445$ f. $799 - 443$

© Frank Schaffer Publications, Inc.   51   FS-32085 Crossword Puzzles

Page 52

Name _____

Fun With Tens

Read each number and find the number word to complete the puzzle.

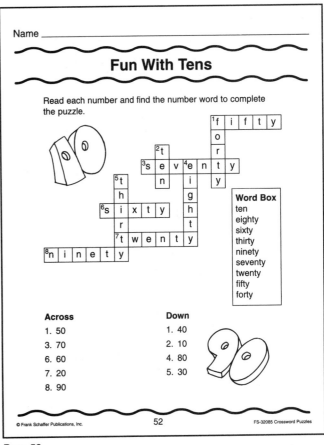

Word Box

ten
eighty
sixty
thirty
ninety
seventy
twenty
fifty
forty

Across

1. 50
3. 70
6. 60
7. 20
8. 90

Down

1. 40
2. 10
4. 80
5. 30

© Frank Schaffer Publications, Inc.   52   FS-32085 Crossword Puzzles

Page 49

Page 50

Page 51

Page 52

117

FS-32085 Crossword Puzzles

Answer Key

At the Zoo

Read the clues. Write the names of the zoo animals in the crossword puzzle.

ZOO

flamingo   koala
monkey   giraffe
seal   penguin
elephant   bear
lion   zebra

Crossword answers:
1. m o n k e y (2-down: o a, 3-across below)
3. l i o n
4. z e b r a (5-down: e, e, a)
6-down: p e n g u i n
7. g i r a f f e
8. f l a m i n g o
9-down: s e a l
10. e l e p h a n t

Across
1. It likes to climb and swing.
3. It is king.
4. It has black and white stripes.
7. It has a very long neck.
8. It has pink feathers.
10. It has a long, long nose.

Down
2. It eats tasty leaves.
5. It has a big fur coat.
6. It lives where it is icy cold.
9. It loves to play and swim in the water.

53   FS-32085 Crossword Puzzles

Page 53

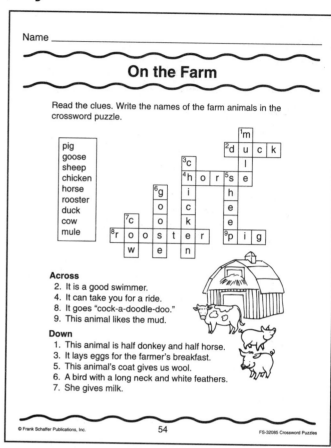

On the Farm

Read the clues. Write the names of the farm animals in the crossword puzzle.

pig
goose
sheep
chicken
horse
rooster
duck
cow
mule

Crossword answers:
1-down: m u l e
2. d u c k
3-down: c h i c k e n
4. h o r s e
5-down: s h e e p
6-down: g o o s e
7-down: c o w
8. r o o s t e r
9. p i g

Across
2. It is a good swimmer.
4. It can take you for a ride.
8. It goes "cock-a-doodle-doo."
9. This animal likes the mud.

Down
1. This animal is half donkey and half horse.
3. It lays eggs for the farmer's breakfast.
5. This animal's coat gives us wool.
6. A bird with a long neck and white feathers.
7. She gives milk.

54   FS-32085 Crossword Puzzles

Page 54

Bugs, Bugs, Bugs

Read the clues. Write the names of the bugs.

wasp
fly
ant
ladybug
cricket
bee
butterfly
caterpillar

Crossword answers:
1. b e e (1-down: b u t t e r f l y)
2-down: c r i c k e t
3-down: w a s p
4. c a t e r p i l l a r
5. f l y
6-down: l
7-down: a n t
6/7. l a d y b u g

Across
1. This is an insect that makes honey.
4. This bug may change into a butterfly.
5. This bug flies around garbage.
6. She wears a red coat with black spots.

Down
1. This bug has beautifully-colored wings.
2. You might hear this bug chirp at night.
3. This stinging insect makes a paper nest.
7. This worker might like your picnic lunch.

55   FS-32085 Crossword Puzzles

Page 55

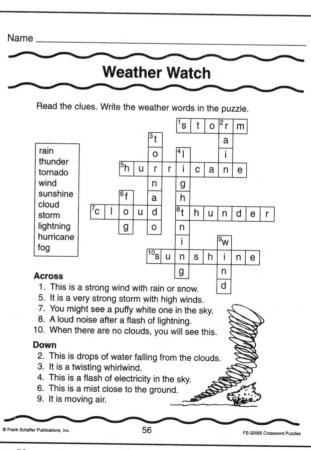

Weather Watch

Read the clues. Write the weather words in the puzzle.

rain
thunder
tornado
wind
sunshine
cloud
storm
lightning
hurricane
fog

Crossword answers:
1. s t o r m (2-down: r a i n)
3-down: t o r n a d o
4-down: l i g h t n i n g
5. h u r r i c a n e
6-down: f o g
7. c l o u d
8. t h u n d e r
9-down: w i n d
10. s u n s h i n e

Across
1. This is a strong wind with rain or snow.
5. It is a very strong storm with high winds.
7. You might see a puffy white one in the sky.
8. A loud noise after a flash of lightning.
10. When there are no clouds, you will see this.

Down
2. This is drops of water falling from the clouds.
3. It is a twisting whirlwind.
4. This is a flash of electricity in the sky.
6. This is a mist close to the ground.
9. It is moving air.

56   FS-32085 Crossword Puzzles

Page 56

FS-32085 Crossword Puzzles

Answer Key

Name

My Body

Read the clues. Write the parts of the body in the puzzle.

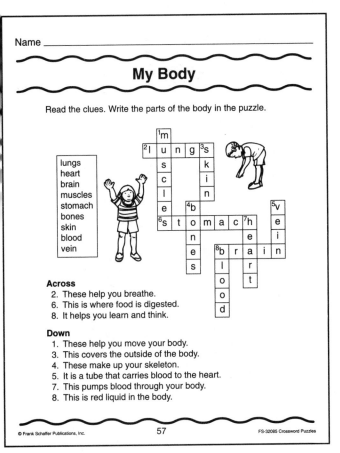

lungs
heart
brain
muscles
stomach
bones
skin
blood
vein

Across
2. These help you breathe.
6. This is where food is digested.
8. It helps you learn and think.

Down
1. These help you move your body.
3. This covers the outside of the body.
4. These make up your skeleton.
5. It is a tube that carries blood to the heart.
7. This pumps blood through your body.
8. This is red liquid in the body.

57
FS-32085 Crossword Puzzles

Page 57

Name

The Ocean

Read the clues. Write the ocean words in the puzzle.

whale   dolphin   diver   lobster
shark   jellyfish   oyster   octopus

Across
3. This animal breathes air and looks like a small whale.
5. This animal lives in a shell.
6. This is a dangerous fish that eats other fish.
7. This ocean animal has eight arms.

Down
1. This mammal looks like a huge fish.
2. It looks like jelly and can sometimes sting.
3. This is a person who dives into the ocean.
4. It has big claws on its front legs.

58
FS-32085 Crossword Puzzles

Page 58

Name

Five Senses

Read the clues. Write the words in the crossword puzzle.

see
eyes
hear
ears
taste
mouth
touch
hands
smell
nose

Across
1. Your hands help you do this.
3. You look at a pretty butterfly with these.
5. Your eyes help you do this.
6. You use your nose to do this.
8. You use these to touch a soft kitten.

Down
1. Your mouth helps you do this.
2. Your ears help you do this.
4. You listen to music with these.
7. You taste your favorite fruit with this.
8. You use this to smell a flower.

59
FS-32085 Crossword Puzzles

Page 59

Name

In Space

Read the clues. Write the space words in the puzzle.

Earth
planets
stars
sun
moon
space shuttle
astronaut
orbit

Across
2. It is the planet we live on.
4. It is the path Earth takes around the sun.
5. This warms Earth and gives it light.
6. It goes around Earth and we see it at night.
7. Astronauts ride this into space.
8. Nine of these go around the sun.

Down
1. There are many of these in the night sky.
3. Someone who travels in space.

60
FS-32085 Crossword Puzzles

Page 60

Answer Key

120

Name _____

Compound Word Fun

Read the clues. Write the compound words in the puzzle.

seashore
rainbow
footprints
sailboat
watermelon
sunburn
sandcastle

Across
1. Your feet make these in the sand.
5. You can swim here.
6. The wind helps this boat move.
7. You don't want to get this at the beach.

Down
2. Look for this in the sky after it rains.
3. You can build one of these in the sand.
4. This tastes good on a hot day.

61

Page 61

Name _____

Words With *ch*, *sh*, *th*, and *wh*

Read the clues. Write the words in the puzzle.

chick
shower
think
whale
cherry
shade
thirteen
white

Across
1. Clouds can be this color.
3. This hatches from an egg.
4. You do this with your brain.
5. It is a spray of water.
6. It is a very big sea mammal.
7. It is a red fruit.

Down
2. The number after twelve.
5. You may find this under a tree.

62

Page 62

Name _____

"S" Blends

Read the clues. Write the words with "s" blends in the puzzle.

score
swim
skate
snake
slide
stars
spoon
smile

Across
1. You glide down this on a playground.
2. Use this to eat your soup.
4. It is a boot with wheels.
6. This is fun to do in a pool.

Down
1. It is a long, thin animal without legs.
2. Keep track of points in a game.
3. These shine in the sky at night.
5. What you do when you are happy.

63

Page 63

Name _____

Homophones Sound Alike

Read the clues. Write the homophones in the puzzle.

ate	eight
two	too
dear	deer
tail	tale
sale	sail

Across
2. A boat can have this.
3. This animal lives in the forest.
5. What you did at lunchtime.
7. This number is one less than three.
8. A squirrel has a long, furry one.

Down
1. This is what you say at the beginning of a letter.
2. A store can have a sign that says this.
4. This is one more than seven.
6. It is a word that means *also*.
7. This is a story.

64

Page 64

Answer Key

Opposites

Name _____

Read the clues. Write the opposites in the crossword puzzle.

Word box: clean, wet, empty, over, inside, under, outside, full, dry, dirty

Across
2. It is the opposite of *under*.
4. It is the opposite of *empty*.
6. It is the opposite of *clean*.
7. It is the opposite of *outside*.
8. It is the opposite of *full*.

Down
1. It is the opposite of *dry*.
2. It is the opposite of *inside*.
3. It is the opposite of *dirty*.
5. It is the opposite of *over*.
6. It is the opposite of *wet*.

© Frank Schaffer Publications, Inc.　65　FS-32085 Crossword Puzzles

Page 65

Long Vowels

Name _____

Read the clues. Write the long vowel words in the puzzle.

Word box: rain, lake, bean, green, tie, pine, toast, pole, glue, tube

Across
2. Eat this at breakfast.
5. This is where a flag goes.
6. It is a vegetable.
7. It is the color of leaves.

Down
1. It is water dropping from clouds.
2. This is what you do to shoelaces.
3. This is what toothpaste comes in.
4. It is fun to swim here.
5. It is a green tree.
7. This will make things stick.

© Frank Schaffer Publications, Inc.　66　FS-32085 Crossword Puzzles

Page 66

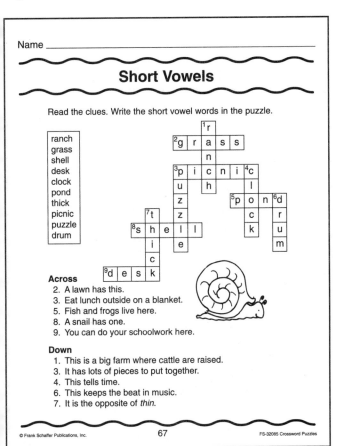

Short Vowels

Name _____

Read the clues. Write the short vowel words in the puzzle.

Word box: ranch, grass, shell, desk, clock, pond, thick, picnic, puzzle, drum

Across
2. A lawn has this.
3. Eat lunch outside on a blanket.
5. Fish and frogs live here.
8. A snail has one.
9. You can do your schoolwork here.

Down
1. This is a big farm where cattle are raised.
3. It has lots of pieces to put together.
4. This tells time.
6. This keeps the beat in music.
7. It is the opposite of *thin*.

© Frank Schaffer Publications, Inc.　67　FS-32085 Crossword Puzzles

Page 67

Parts of a Book

Name _____

Read the clues. Write the parts of a book in the puzzle.

Word box: title, author, illustrator, publisher, date, pages, words, pictures, cover, jacket

Across
5. This is a person who draws the pictures.
7. This is the name of the book.
9. The pieces of paper in a book.
10. The writing in a book.

Down
1. The year the book was made.
2. The drawings or photos in a book.
3. The company that made the book.
4. The outside front and back of the book.
6. The person who wrote the book.
8. A paper cover on the outside of a book.

© Frank Schaffer Publications, Inc.　68　FS-32085 Crossword Puzzles

Page 68

© Frank Schaffer Publications, Inc.

121

FS-32085 Crossword Puzzles

Answer Key

Frog and Toad Together

Name _____

Have you read the book *Frog and Toad Together* by Arnold Lobel? Read the clues. Write the words from the story in the crossword puzzle.

Word box:
list
wind
garden
seeds
cookies
birds
brave
dream
wonderful

Puzzle answers:
3. cookies
4. birds
6. brave
8. dream
9. wind
(Down) 1. list, 2. wonderful, 5. seeds, 7. garden

Across
3. You need will power not to eat these.
4. They might like to eat some cookies.
6. This is the opposite of *afraid*.
8. This is what Toad did when he was sleeping.
9. This can blow away your list of things to do.

Down
1. This is something you write.
2. What you might call the greatest toad in all the world.
5. These take some time to grow into flowers.
7. This is where you plant seeds.

Page 69

The Gingerbread Man

Name _____

Do you know the story of The Gingerbread Man? Read the clues. Write the words from the story in the puzzle.

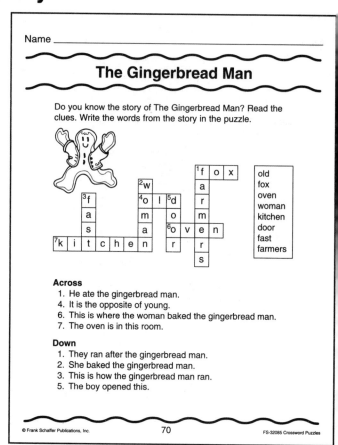

Puzzle answers:
1. fox
4. old
6. oven
7. kitchen
(Down) 2. woman, 3. fast, 5. door, and farmers

Word box:
old
fox
oven
woman
kitchen
door
fast
farmers

Across
1. He ate the gingerbread man.
4. It is the opposite of young.
6. This is where the woman baked the gingerbread man.
7. The oven is in this room.

Down
1. They ran after the gingerbread man.
2. She baked the gingerbread man.
3. This is how the gingerbread man ran.
5. The boy opened this.

Page 70

Blueberries for Sal

Name _____

Have you read the book *Blueberries for Sal* by Robert McCloskey? Read the clues. Write the words from the story in the crossword puzzle.

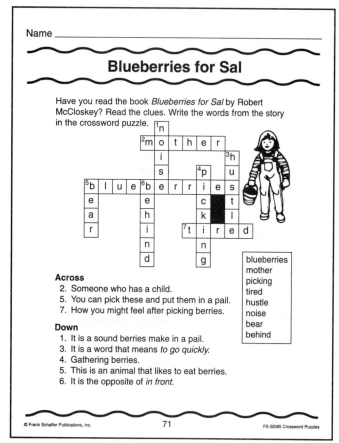

Puzzle answers:
2. mother
5. blueberries
7. tired
(Down) 1. noise, 3. hustle, 4. picking, 5. bear, 6. behind

Word box:
blueberries
mother
picking
tired
hustle
noise
bear
behind

Across
2. Someone who has a child.
5. You can pick these and put them in a pail.
7. How you might feel after picking berries.

Down
1. It is a sound berries make in a pail.
3. It is a word that means *to go quickly*.
4. Gathering berries.
5. This is an animal that likes to eat berries.
6. It is the opposite of *in front*.

Page 71

Nursery Rhymes

Name _____

Read the clues. Write the nursery rhyme words in the puzzle.

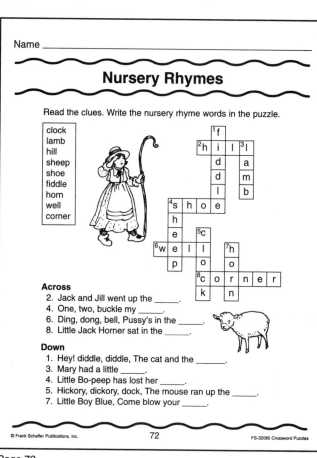

Word box:
clock
lamb
hill
sheep
shoe
fiddle
horn
well
corner

Puzzle answers:
2. hill
4. shoe
6. well
8. corner
(Down) 1. fiddle, 3. lamb, 4. sheep, 5. clock, 7. horn

Across
2. Jack and Jill went up the _____.
4. One, two, buckle my _____.
6. Ding, dong, bell, Pussy's in the _____.
8. Little Jack Horner sat in the _____.

Down
1. Hey! diddle, diddle, The cat and the _____.
3. Mary had a little _____.
4. Little Bo-peep has lost her _____.
5. Hickory, dickory, dock, The mouse ran up the _____.
7. Little Boy Blue, Come blow your _____.

Page 72

Answer Key

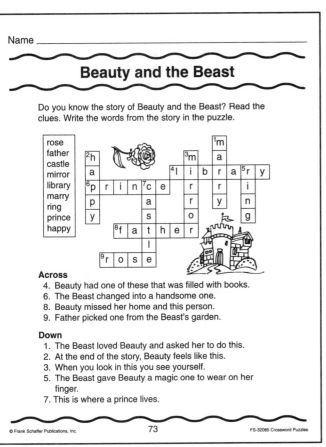

Name _____

Beauty and the Beast

Do you know the story of Beauty and the Beast? Read the clues. Write the words from the story in the puzzle.

Word list: rose, father, castle, mirror, library, marry, ring, prince, happy

Crossword answers:
- 1 down: marry
- 2 down: happy
- 3 down: mirror
- 4 across: library
- 5 down: ring
- 6 across: prince
- 7 down: castle
- 8 across: father
- 9 across: rose

Across
4. Beauty had one of these that was filled with books.
6. The Beast changed into a handsome one.
8. Beauty missed her home and this person.
9. Father picked one from the Beast's garden.

Down
1. The Beast loved Beauty and asked her to do this.
2. At the end of the story, Beauty feels like this.
3. When you look in this you see yourself.
5. The Beast gave Beauty a magic one to wear on her finger.
7. This is where a prince lives.

© Frank Schaffer Publications, Inc.   73   FS-32085 Crossword Puzzles

Page 73

Name _____

The Elves and the Shoemaker

Do you know the story of the Elves and the Shoemaker? Read the clues. Write the words from the story in the puzzle.

Crossword answers:
- 1 down: hammer
- 2 across: clothes
- 3 down: shoemaker
- 4 across: midnight
- 5 across: leather
- 6 across: work
- 7 across: elves

Word list: shoemaker, wife, midnight, elves, clothes, leather, hammer, work

Across
2. The shoemaker's wife made these for the elves to wear.
4. The elves came at this time of night.
5. The shoemaker cut this to make shoes.
6. This is the opposite of *play*.
7. These are magical little people.

Down
1. This is a tool for making shoes.
3. This is a person who makes shoes.
6. The shoemaker was married to her.

© Frank Schaffer Publications, Inc.   74   FS-32085 Crossword Puzzles

Page 74

Name _____

The Three Bears

Do you know the story of the Three Bears? Read the clues. Write the words from the story in the puzzle.

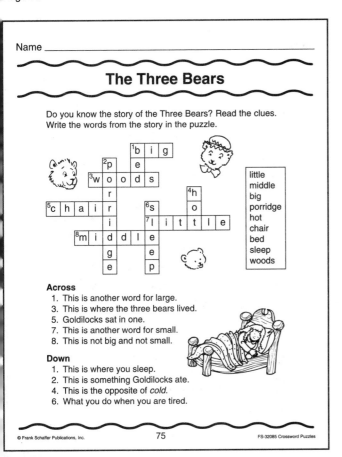

Crossword answers:
- 1 across: big
- 2 down: porridge
- 3 across: woods
- 4 down: hot
- 5 across: chair
- 6 down: sleep
- 7 across: little
- 8 across: middle

Word list: little, middle, big, porridge, hot, chair, bed, sleep, woods

Across
1. This is another word for large.
3. This is where the three bears lived.
5. Goldilocks sat in one.
7. This is another word for small.
8. This is not big and not small.

Down
1. This is where you sleep.
2. This is something Goldilocks ate.
4. This is the opposite of *cold*.
6. What you do when you are tired.

© Frank Schaffer Publications, Inc.   75   FS-32085 Crossword Puzzles

Page 75

Name _____

Making Music

Read the clues. Write the music words in the puzzle.

Crossword answers:
- 1 down: violin
- 2 down: listen
- 3 across: piano
- 4 down: guitar
- 5 across: note
- 6 across: horn
- 7 across: drum
- 8 down: music
- 9 across: bells

Word list: drum, horn, violin, piano, guitar, note, music, listen, bells

Across
3. This instrument has black and white keys.
5. It is a musical sound.
6. You blow into this instrument.
7. Strike this instrument to make sounds.
9. Ring these to make sounds.

Down
1. You play the strings on this instrument with a bow.
2. People do this when they hear music.
4. An electric one is used for rock and roll.
8. It is another word for beautiful sounds.

© Frank Schaffer Publications, Inc.   76   FS-32085 Crossword Puzzles

Page 76

Answer Key

Moving to Music

Read the clues. Write the movement words in the crossword puzzle.

stretch
move
dance
leap
glide
step
skip
whirl
pose

Across
3. This is another word for walk.
6. You turn fast when you do this.
7. It is a jump.
8. You do this when you move to music.

Down
1. You do this when you go from one place to another.
2. Reach out and make your body fill more space.
3. You do this when you move with little leaps.
4. You do this when you stand very still.
5. This means moving smoothly.

77   FS-32085 Crossword Puzzles

Page 77

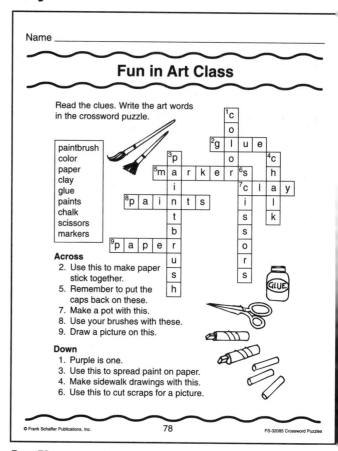

Fun in Art Class

Read the clues. Write the art words in the crossword puzzle.

paintbrush
color
paper
clay
glue
paints
chalk
scissors
markers

Across
2. Use this to make paper stick together.
5. Remember to put the caps back on these.
7. Make a pot with this.
8. Use your brushes with these.
9. Draw a picture on this.

Down
1. Purple is one.
3. Use this to spread paint on paper.
4. Make sidewalk drawings with this.
6. Use this to cut scraps for a picture.

78   FS-32085 Crossword Puzzles

Page 78

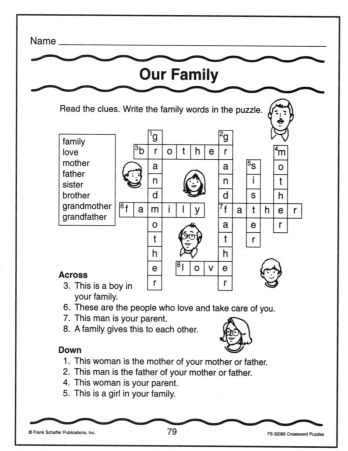

Our Family

Read the clues. Write the family words in the puzzle.

family
love
mother
father
sister
brother
grandmother
grandfather

Across
3. This is a boy in your family.
6. These are the people who love and take care of you.
7. This man is your parent.
8. A family gives this to each other.

Down
1. This woman is the mother of your mother or father.
2. This man is the father of your mother or father.
4. This woman is your parent.
5. This is a girl in your family.

79   FS-32085 Crossword Puzzles

Page 79

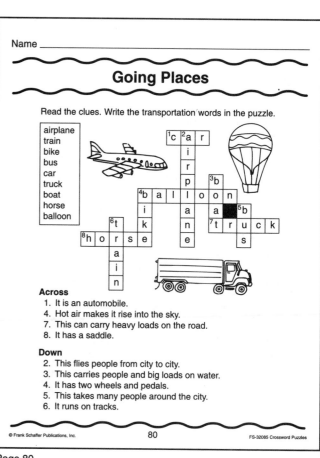

Going Places

Read the clues. Write the transportation words in the puzzle.

airplane
train
bike
bus
car
truck
boat
horse
balloon

Across
1. It is an automobile.
4. Hot air makes it rise into the sky.
7. This can carry heavy loads on the road.
8. It has a saddle.

Down
2. This flies people from city to city.
3. This carries people and big loads on water.
4. It has two wheels and pedals.
5. This takes many people around the city.
6. It runs on tracks.

80   FS-32085 Crossword Puzzles

Page 80

FS-32085 Crossword Puzzles

Answer Key

At a Powwow

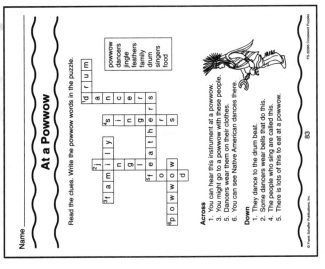

Name _____

Read the clues. Write the powwow words in the puzzle.

Word Box: powwow, dancers, jingle, feathers, family, drum, singers, food

Across
1. You can hear this instrument at a powwow.
3. You might go to a powwow with these people.
5. Dancers wear them on their clothes.
6. You can see Native American dances there.

Down
1. They dance to the drum beat.
2. Some dancers wear bells that do this.
4. The people who sing are called this.
5. There is lots of this to eat at a powwow.

83

© Frank Schaffer Publications, Inc.

FS-32085 Crossword Puzzles

Page 83

Winter

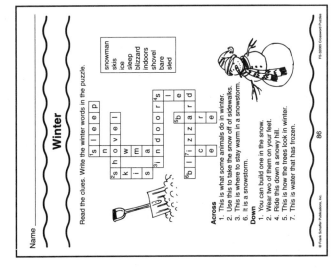

Name _____

Read the clues. Write the winter words in the puzzle.

Word Box: snowman, skis, ice, sleep, blizzard, indoors, shovel, bare, sled

Across
1. This is what some animals do in winter.
2. Use this to take the snow off of sidewalks.
3. This is where to stay warm in a snowstorm.
6. It is a snowstorm.

Down
1. You can build one in the snow.
2. Wear two of them on your feet.
4. Ride this down a snowy hill.
5. This is how the trees look in winter.
7. This is water that has frozen.

86

© Frank Schaffer Publications, Inc.

FS-32085 Crossword Puzzles

Page 86

At School

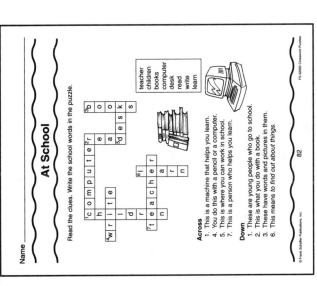

Name _____

Read the clues. Write the school words in the puzzle.

Word Box: teacher, children, books, computer, desk, read, write, learn

Across
1. This is a machine that helps you learn.
4. You do this with a pencil or a computer.
5. This is where you can work in school.
7. This is a person who helps you learn.

Down
1. These are young people who go to school.
2. This is what you do with a book.
3. These have words and pictures in them.
6. This means to find out about things.

82

© Frank Schaffer Publications, Inc.

FS-32085 Crossword Puzzles

Page 82

Animal Homes

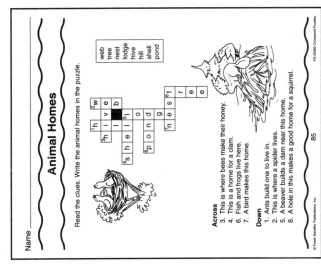

Name _____

Read the clues. Write the animal homes in the puzzle.

Word Box: web, tree, nest, lodge, hive, hill, shell, pond

Across
3. This is where bees make their honey.
4. This is a home for a clam.
6. Fish and frogs live here.
7. A bird makes this home.

Down
1. Ants build one to live in.
2. This is where a spider lives.
5. A beaver builds a dam near this home.
8. A hole in this makes a good home for a squirrel.

85

© Frank Schaffer Publications, Inc.

FS-32085 Crossword Puzzles

Page 85

Around the City

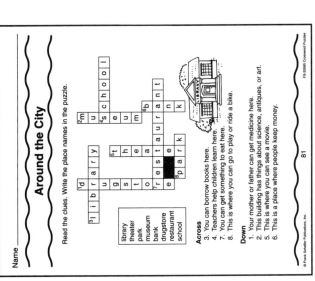

Name _____

Read the clues. Write the place names in the puzzle.

Word Box: library, theater, park, museum, bank, drugstore, restaurant, school

Across
3. You can borrow books here.
4. Teachers help children learn here.
7. You can get something to eat here.
8. This is where you can go to play or ride a bike.

Down
1. Your mother or father can get medicine here.
2. This building has things about science, antiques, or art.
5. This is where you can see a movie.
6. This is a place where people keep money.

81

© Frank Schaffer Publications, Inc.

FS-32085 Crossword Puzzles

Page 81

Around the World

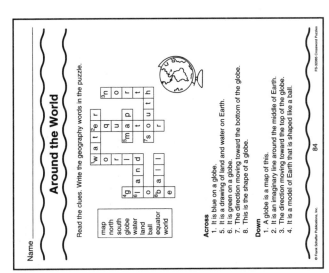

Name _____

Read the clues. Write the geography words in the puzzle.

Word Box: map, north, south, globe, water, land, ball, equator, world

Across
1. It is blue on a globe.
5. It is a drawing of land and water on Earth.
6. It is green on a globe.
7. The direction moving toward the bottom of the globe.
8. This is the shape of a globe.

Down
1. A globe is a map of this.
2. It is an imaginary line around the middle of Earth.
3. The direction moving toward the top of the globe.
4. It is a model of Earth that is shaped like a ball.

84

© Frank Schaffer Publications, Inc.

FS-32085 Crossword Puzzles

Page 84

Answer Key

Fall

Name _____

Read the clues. Write the fall words in the crossword puzzle.

| leaves |
| pumpkin |
| apples |
| moon |
| yellow |
| squirrels |
| geese |
| rake |

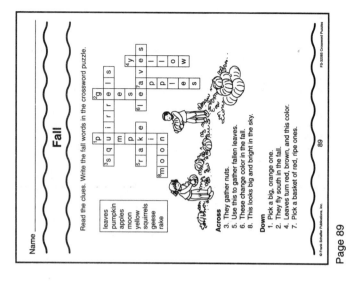

Crossword answers:
- ⁴yellow
- leaves
- ⁷plow
- ²geese
- mms
- ³squirrels
- ⁵leaves
- p p
- ⁶rake
- i i
- ⁸moon

Across
3. They gather nuts.
5. Use this to gather fallen leaves.
6. These change color in the fall.
8. This looks big and bright in the sky.

Down
1. Pick a big, orange one.
2. They fly south in the fall.
4. Leaves turn red, brown, and this color.
7. Pick a basket of red, ripe ones.

© Frank Schaffer Publications, Inc.

89

FS-32085 Crossword Puzzles

Page 89

Every Day Is Earth Day

Name _____

Read the clues. Write the Earth words in the crossword puzzle.

| paper |
| plant |
| recycle |
| litter |
| care |
| reuse |
| clean |
| walk |

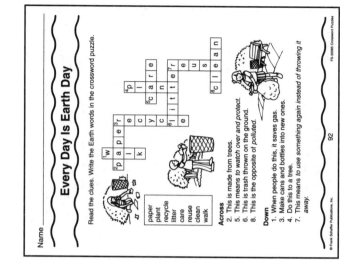

Crossword answers:
- clean
- care
- ⁷reuse
- ⁵care
- ⁶litter
- ²paper
- ³recycle
- w l
- walk

Across
2. This is made from trees.
5. This means to *watch over and protect.*
6. This is trash thrown on the ground.
8. This is the opposite of *polluted.*

Down
1. When people do this, it saves gas.
3. Make cans and bottles into new ones.
4. Do this to a tree.
7. This means to *use something again instead of throwing it away.*

© Frank Schaffer Publications, Inc.

92

FS-32085 Crossword Puzzles

Page 92

Summer

Name _____

Read the clues. Write the summer words in the puzzle.

| green |
| birds |
| butterflies |
| bees |
| hot |
| sunny |
| swim |
| picnic |

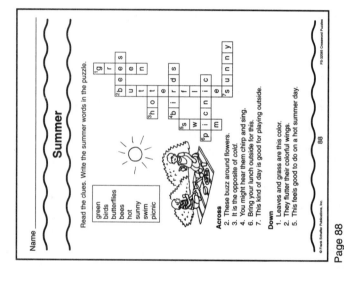

Crossword answers:
- ¹green
- ²bees
- ³hot
- ⁴birds
- sunny
- ⁵swim
- ⁶picnic

Across
2. These buzz around flowers.
3. It is the opposite of *cold.*
4. You might hear them chirp and sing.
6. Bring your lunch outside for this.
7. This kind of day is good for playing outside.

Down
1. Leaves and grass are this color.
2. They flutter their colorful wings.
5. This feels good to do on a hot summer day.

© Frank Schaffer Publications, Inc.

88

FS-32085 Crossword Puzzles

Page 88

Bird-watching

Name _____

Read the clues. Write the bird words in the crossword puzzle.

| feathers |
| nest |
| egg |
| fly |
| flock |
| birdhouse |
| wings |
| hatched |
| sing |

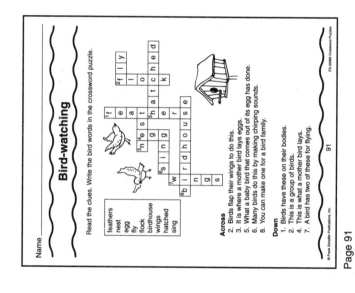

Crossword answers:
- ²fly
- ³hatched
- ¹feathers
- ⁴nest
- ⁵sing
- ⁷birdhouse

Across
2. Birds flap their wings to do this.
3. It is where a mother bird lays eggs.
5. What a baby bird that comes out of its egg has done.
6. Many birds do this by making chirping sounds.
8. You can make one for a bird family.

Down
1. Birds have these on their bodies.
2. This is a group of birds.
4. This is what a mother bird lays.
7. A bird has two of these for flying.

© Frank Schaffer Publications, Inc.

91

FS-32085 Crossword Puzzles

Page 91

Spring

Name _____

Read the clues. Write the spring words in the puzzle.

| buds |
| warmer |
| flowers |
| caterpillar |
| windy |
| rainy |
| kite |
| outdoors |

Crossword answers:
- ²warmer
- ⁴flowers
- ⁵kite
- ³flowers
- ⁸rainy
- ⁶buds

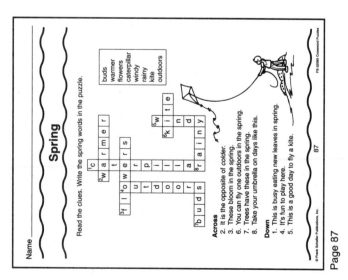

Across
2. It is the opposite of *colder.*
4. These bloom in the spring.
6. You can fly one outdoors in the spring.
7. Trees have these in the spring.
8. Take your umbrella on days like this.

Down
1. This is busy eating new leaves in spring.
4. It's fun to play here.
5. This is a good day to fly a kite.

© Frank Schaffer Publications, Inc.

87

FS-32085 Crossword Puzzles

Page 87

The Calendar

Name _____

Read the clues. Write the calendar words in the crossword puzzle.

| days |
| week |
| month |
| year |
| calendar |
| holiday |
| birthday |
| time |

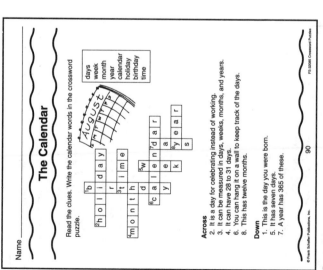

Crossword answers:
- ²holiday
- ³month
- ⁵time
- ⁶calendar
- ⁷year
- ⁴month

Across
2. It is a day for celebrating instead of working.
3. It can be measured in days, weeks, months, and years.
4. It can have 28 to 31 days.
6. You can hang it on a wall to keep track of the days.
8. This has twelve months.

Down
1. This is the day you were born.
5. It has seven days.
7. A year has 365 of these.

© Frank Schaffer Publications, Inc.

90

FS-32085 Crossword Puzzles

Page 90

© Frank Schaffer Publications, Inc.

126

FS-32085 Crossword Puzzles

Answer Key

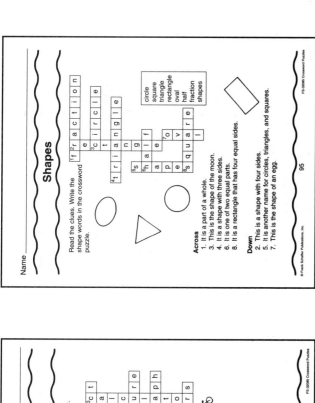

Shapes

Read the clues. Write the shape words in the crossword puzzle.

Word box: circle / square / triangle / rectangle / oval / half / fraction / shapes

Across
1. It is a part of a whole.
3. This is the shape of the moon.
4. It is a shape with three sides.
6. It is one of two equal parts.
8. It is a rectangle that has four equal sides.

Down
2. This is a shape with four sides.
5. It is another name for circles, triangles, and squares.
7. This is the shape of an egg.

Page 95

95

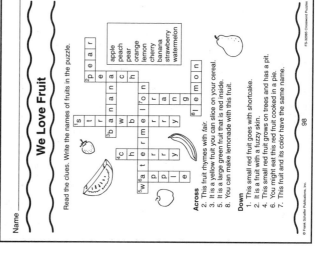

We Love Fruit

Read the clues. Write the names of fruits in the puzzle.

Word box: apple / peach / pear / orange / lemon / cherry / banana / strawberry / watermelon

Across
2. This fruit rhymes with *fair.*
3. It is a yellow fruit you can slice on your cereal.
5. It is a large green fruit that is red inside.
8. You can make lemonade with this fruit.

Down
1. This small red fruit goes with shortcake.
2. It is a fruit with a fuzzy skin.
4. This small red fruit grows on trees and has a pit.
6. You might eat this red fruit cooked in a pie.
7. This fruit and its color have the same name.

Page 98

98

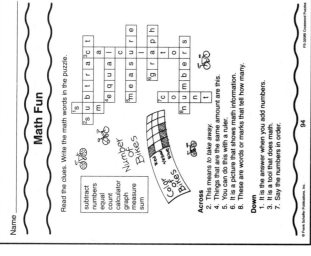

Math Fun

Read the clues. Write the math words in the puzzle.

Word box: subtract / numbers / equal / count / calculator / graph / measure / sum

Across
2. This means *to take away.*
4. Things that are the same amount are this.
5. You can do this with a ruler.
6. It is a picture that shows math information.
8. These are words or marks that tell how many.

Down
1. It is the answer when you add numbers.
3. It is a tool that does math.
7. Say the numbers in order.

Page 94

94

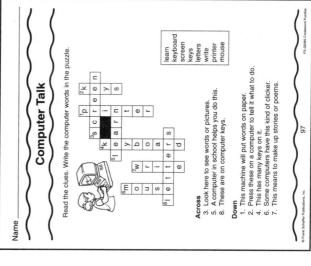

Computer Talk

Read the clues. Write the computer words in the puzzle.

Word box: learn / keyboard / screen / keys / letters / write / printer / mouse

Across
3. Look here to see words or pictures.
5. A computer in school helps you do this.
8. These are on computer keys.

Down
1. This machine will put words on paper.
2. Press these on a computer to tell it what to do.
4. This has many keys on it.
6. Some computers have this kind of clicker.
7. This means to make up stories or poems.

Page 97

97

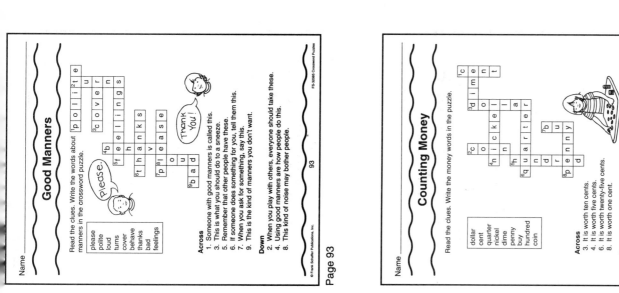

Good Manners

Read the clues. Write the words about manners in the crossword puzzle.

Word box: please / polite / loud / turns / cover / behave / thanks / bad / feelings

Across
1. Someone with good manners is called this.
3. This is what you should do to a sneeze.
5. Remember that other people have these.
6. If someone does something for you, tell them this.
7. When you ask for something, say this.
9. This is the kind of manners you don't want.

Down
2. When you play with others, everyone should take these.
4. Using good manners are how people do this.
8. This kind of noise may bother people.

Page 93

93

Counting Money

Read the clues. Write the money words in the puzzle.

Word box: dollar / cent / quarter / nickel / dime / penny / buy / hundred / coin

Across
3. It is worth ten cents.
4. It is worth five cents.
6. It is worth twenty-five cents.
8. It is worth one cent.

Down
1. It is another name for a penny.
2. It is another name for a dime, nickel, or penny.
3. It equals one hundred cents.
5. This is how many pennies there are in a dollar.
7. You can save your money or you can do this.

Page 96

96

FS-32085 Crossword Puzzles

Answer Key

Page 101 — Sports

Name _____

Sports

Read the clues. Write the sports in the crossword puzzle.

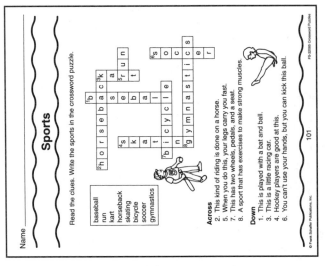

Word list: baseball, run, kart, horseback, skating, bicycle, soccer, gymnastics

Across
2. This kind of riding is done on a horse.
5. When you do this, your legs carry you fast.
7. This has two wheels, pedals, and a seat.
8. A sport that has exercises to make strong muscles.

Down
1. This is played with a bat and ball.
3. This is a little racing car.
4. Hockey players are good at this.
6. You can't use your hands, but you can kick this ball.

101 — FS-32085 Crossword Puzzles

Page 104 — The Circus

Name _____

The Circus

Read the clues. Write the circus words in the puzzle.

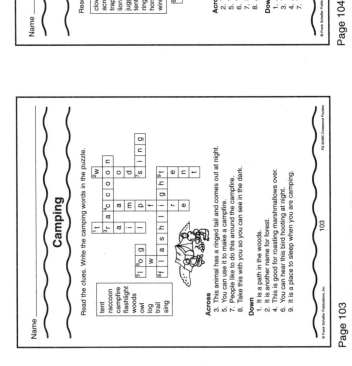

Word list: clown, acrobat, trapeze, lion, juggler, tent, ringmaster, horseback, wire

Across
2. This person can swing on a trapeze.
5. This person is in charge of the circus ring.
6. This person wears a funny nose and a painted smile.
7. It is like a swing.
8. An acrobat can walk on one high up in the air.

Down
1. Acrobats stand while riding like this.
3. This person can do tricks with balls.
4. A trainer works with this animal.
7. The circus is inside of this.

104 — FS-32085 Crossword Puzzles

Page 100 — Playground Fun

Name _____

Playground Fun

Read the clues. Write the playground words in the puzzle.

Word list: tag, slide, swing, climb, friends, recess, rope, hopscotch, sand

Across
5. It is a break from schoolwork.
6. This is how you go up a slide.
7. In this game, you run and touch someone.
8. If it's slippery, you'll go down fast.

Down
1. You can jump it.
2. To play this game, draw it on a sidewalk.
3. They are people you like to play with.
4. Sit on this and pump your legs to move.
8. You can dig in this and make roads.

100 — FS-32085 Crossword Puzzles

Page 103 — Camping

Name _____

Camping

Read the clues. Write the camping words in the puzzle.

Word list: tent, raccoon, campfire, flashlight, woods, owl, log, trail, sing

Across
3. This animal has a ringed tail and comes out at night.
5. You can use it to make a campfire.
7. People like to do this around the campfire.
8. Take this with you so you can see in the dark.

Down
1. It is a path in the woods.
2. It is another name for forest.
4. This is good for roasting marshmallows over.
6. You can hear this bird hooting at night.
9. It is a place to sleep when you are camping.

103 — FS-32085 Crossword Puzzles

Page 99 — In the Garden

Name _____

In the Garden

Read the clues. Write the garden words in the puzzle.

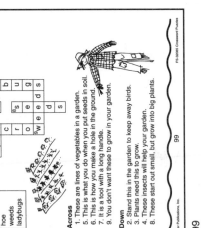

Word list: scarecrow, dig, rows, plant, seeds, water, hoe, weeds, ladybugs

Across
1. These are lines of vegetables in a garden.
5. This is what you do when you put seeds in soil.
6. This is how you make a hole in the ground.
7. It is a tool with a long handle.
9. You don't want these to grow in your garden.

Down
2. Stand this in the garden to keep away birds.
3. Plants need this to grow.
4. These insects will help your garden.
8. These start out small, but grow into big plants.

99 — FS-32085 Crossword Puzzles

Page 102 — In the Snow

Name _____

In the Snow

Read the clues. Write the snow words in the crossword puzzle.

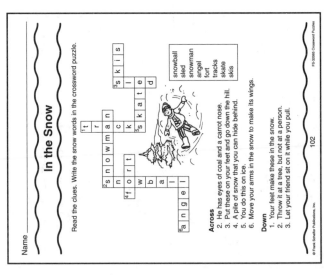

Word list: snowball, sled, snowman, angel, fort, tracks, skate, skis

Across
2. He has eyes of coal and a carrot nose.
3. Put these on your feet and go down the hill.
4. A pile of snow that you can hide behind.
5. You do this on ice.
6. Move your arms in the snow to make its wings.

Down
1. Your feet make these in the snow.
2. Throw it at a tree, but not at a person.
3. Let your friend sit on it while you pull.

102 — FS-32085 Crossword Puzzles